the poem. He shows how this subtle dimension of *Paradise Lost* accounts in large part for its power. Underlying the whole treatment is an assumption that during the act of composition a good poet's mind is often stirred to its depths and registers with astonishing fidelity what is happening on all levels of his psyche, conscious and unconscious.

Wayne Shumaker is Professor of English at the University of California, Berkeley.

UNPREMEDITATED VERSE

If answerable stile I can obtaine
Of my Celestial Patroness, who deignes
Her nightly visitation unimplor'd,
And dictates to me slumbring, or inspires
Easie my unpremeditated Verse . . .

PARADISE LOST, IX, 20-24

UNPREMEDITATED VERSE:

FEELING AND PERCEPTION IN

PARADISE LOST

BY WAYNE SHUMAKER

PRINCETON, NEW JERSEY

PRINCETON UNIVERSITY PRESS

1967

Publication of this book has been aided
by the Whitney Darrow Publication Reserve Fund
of Princeton University Press

Printed in the United States of America
by Princeton University Press

PREFACE

Although the intention and plan of the present study are explained from chapter to chapter, a quick overview of what is to follow may be helpful.

With regard to subject matter, the study is divided into roughly equal halves, the first focusing on the embodiment of feelings in *Paradise Lost*, the second on the embodiment of perceptions. The first and last chapters, however, treat both perceptions and feelings: the first because at the level of generalization necessary to discuss the impact of "myth" on human consciousness distinctions between what is perceived and what is felt are not easily drawn, and the last because I wanted to suggest how analysis of the irrational element in literature—that is, the parts of literature which are neither deductively nor inductively structured—might proceed when the analysis was guided not by method but by poetic content. By "feeling," or alternatively, "affect," is meant whatever has emotive quality—for example, attitudinal biases and yearnings or aversions, however low-keyed and unconscious. Although the importance of these to poetry has always been given theoretical recognition, in recent years an emphasis on "meaning" has tended to imply that poets are especially deep thinkers. I grant happily that what they say often has special profundity, but I am convinced that this is achieved less because the discursive intellects of poets have exceptional acuity than because they allow all the parts of their minds, including direct intuition and sensory perception, unusually free play. If this is true of Milton, who together with Lucretius is almost an archetype of the philosopher-poet, it is true of other poets

a fortiori. So much for feelings. Of perceptions I have separated out for expanded treatment only three major kinds,
visual, auditory, and what I have called somatic. Concerning
the last I myself have some uncertainty; and no doubt other
varieties exist besides the commonly accepted ones of touch,
taste, and smell, which appear to play a comparatively minor
role in literature except on special occasions (for instance, in the
banquet scene of *Paradise Regained*). Motor imagery is an
obvious possibility, but it slipped so frequently into the discussion in byways that it has not been allowed a chapter to
itself.

From the point of view of method, a second structure over-
laps the one just described. Chapters I and II have to do with
the whole poem viewed from particular perspectives; Chapter
III is intended to render initially plausible the kinds of
analysis next to be attempted; and Chapters IV-IX treat in
constantly changing ways successive two-book sections of the
epic. I have preferred taking blocks of the poetic material as
they came to searching for passages obviously rich in the
appropriate kinds of poetic data because I wished to discover
not what bravura effects Milton could attain but how he
regularly and characteristically wrote.

In order to avoid misunderstanding I should like to make
three explicit disavowals. The first is a denial that Milton
consciously intended all the effects asserted to be present. Fitnesses are often recognized by a part of the poet's mind which
not only is nondiscursive but feels no strong pressure to become discursively self-conscious. For a defense of this claim
I must refer the interested reader to my *Literature and the
Irrational*,[1] where the principle is argued in Chapters I and
II and made basic to the remainder of the discussion. Here I
must limit myself to remarking that language is an instrument so sensitive that it not only reveals qualities of which

[1] Prentice-Hall, 1960; Washington Square Press, 1966.

users are unaware but sometimes betrays attitudes they attempt deliberately to hide. I remember a number of years ago being asked by a colleague why I had been so angry when I wrote him a brief note. I had indeed been angry but thought I had succeeded, by revisions, in making the note tonally colorless; and when I looked at my copy, I was unable to guess what effect of rhythm or diction had betrayed me. Secondly, I am not a Jungian and do not believe that the mental experiences of ancestors can be inherited; indeed, I am not even a Freudian, though I honor Freud and think many of his insights brilliant. And finally, the lack of consistent historical orientation in what follows (except Chapter I, where the temporal depth is so great that it must be handled in odd ways) does not imply disesteem of historical scholarship. I value history and read many kinds of it *con amore*; it simply happens that for some time I have been embarked on a critical task which requires a different emphasis.

The reason I have undertaken the task deserves brief comment. If I know myself at all, I am not temperamentally inclined to mysticism. On the contrary, I am instinctively and strongly repelled by magic, numerology, astrology, theosophy, palmistry, and the like and can begin to take an interest in them only after the possibility of grasping them conceptually has dawned on me (as, for example, when I learned that in magic "Things which have once been in contact with each other continue to affect each other even when separated"). Yet for some time I have been convinced that modern criticism, which in many respects is the most subtle and penetrating the world has yet known, has obscured an extraordinary capacity of poetry to make accessible to contemplation, and hence to cognition, those parts of our total psychic activity which are not rationally articulated. I trust that the rational articulation of my own thought will quickly become evident.

The exploitation of special interests has meant inevitably

that the discussion attempted here could not be exhaustive—
a fault which matters less because in recent years so many
enviably good books have been written about *Paradise Lost*.
My hope has been to supplement, not to supplant, whatever
total understanding of the epic the reader has already achieved.
In the fact of the poem's tough rationality I have found not
discouragement but an exceptional opportunity to test my
hypotheses.

All Milton quotations are taken from Helen Darbishire's
The Poetical Works of John Milton (London: Oxford University Press, 1958). My thanks are due to the publishers for
permission to quote from that edition.

Although I have sought comparatively little advice, certain
acknowledgments are due. A different version of Chapter I
was discussed vigorously at the Modern Language Association
meeting in 1960 and subsequently published in December
1961 in the *Bucknell Review*. For permission to reprint what
is identical in that version and the present one I am grateful.
Professor Kakuaki Saito, of International Christian University, Tokyo, made helpful comments on Chapter VII while
I was acting as director of the University of California Study
Center at that institution; I have benefited by advice obtained
through the Princeton University Press; and the members of
my fall 1965 seminar in Milton and His Contemporaries at
the Berkeley campus of the University of California heard
and discussed Chapters I, VI, VII, and VIII. No one's approval
but my own, however, is to be inferred. Finally, I owe a special
debt to Mrs. Natalie Sands Sousa, who as my research as-
sistant showed admirable skill and learning in selecting and
typing up on cards the words and phrases cited in Chapters
IV and V, and to Arthur J. Weiner, who checked most of the
relatively inaccessible references.

Berkeley   WAYNE SHUMAKER
January 12, 1967

CONTENTS

UNPREMEDITATED VERSE

....

CHAPTER I

PARADISE LOST

AS MYTH

That *Paradise Lost* makes frequent allusions to myths, classical and other, everyone is aware; but that the poem itself *is* myth seems often to escape notice.[1] Its Christian subject matter is too close even to twentieth century readers to be viewed as existing on the same plane with interesting but fantastic legends about beings called Prometheus and Wotan and the Cannibal-at-the-North-End-of-the-World. Moreover, the tone of Milton's epic, unlike that—for example—of Ovid's *Metamorphoses*, is pervasively and weightily rational. The discursive explanations tempt us to criticize the events not as fiction but as alleged truth. Yet all myth while it flourishes is believed, and many myths, including those of the Greeks, have been rationalized. In a precise sense, "myths" are in fact stories which are, or were, credited as divine history. We do not respond appropriately to Milton's poem if we do not, however else we may react to it, also grant it suspended disbelief as a record of divine events which have determined the nature of the world and the human situation as we experience them daily. I propose to inquire briefly whether the poem's extraordinary power, which overwhelms some readers and provokes others to indignant resistance, does not derive partly from its capacity, as myth, to stimulate the deepest and most

---

[1] *Paradise Lost as "Myth,"* by Isabel Gamble MacCaffrey, Cambridge: Harvard University Press, 1959, suggests that an awareness of the epic's mythical character is emerging, as do also certain writings of Northrop Frye. Mrs. MacCaffrey's treatment is quite different, however, from that attempted here.

3

primitive layers of human feeling; but I shall do so—by intention, at least—utterly without mysticism and without wishing to imply that any psychic phenomena are ultimately beyond rational understanding.

In preliterate societies, it appears both from the oldest surviving literary documents and from anthropological observations of existing savages, speculative problems tend regularly to be solved not in terms of physical or biological law but of dramatic incident, of story. The fact is too well known to require extended illustration. Among the Greeks, the Romans, the Japanese, the Hindus, the Persians, and the Germanic peoples, as well as among contemporary savages, the question "Why?" appears regularly to have been answered, at remote periods, in terms of *who* and *how*. Why does the cocoanut shell have three small depressions at one end? The markings, say the Polynesian Mangaians, are the eyes and mouth of the eel, Ina, from whose decapitated and buried head the cocoanut tree sprang.[2] Why is Cassiopeia visible in the northern sky? It was once a girl, whom Poseidon made into a constellation because of her treachery. Where did a group of Japanese islands come from? They were born of Her Augustness the Female-Who-Invites after cohabitation with His Augustness the Male-Who-Invites.[3] The world is not dead and insensate for "natural" man, but permeated with energy and will; and story—myth—is an important means by which he becomes cognitively at home in his environment.

The inclination of modern children also to explain their environment by means of tell-me-why stories suggests that the primitive tendency has a biological root. We have all been children, if not savages with hair strings about our waists; and Jean Piaget, in *The Language and Thought of the Child,*

[2] William Wyatt Gill, *Myths and Songs from the South Pacific,* London: Henry S. King & Co., 1876, pp. 77-79.

[3] Basil Hall Chamberlain, *Translation of "Ko-Ji-Ki" (Records of Ancient Matters),* 2d edn., Kobe: The Asiatic Society of Japan, 1932, pp. 24ff.

has shown that the six-year-old "still openly regards as animated" such objects as "stars, fire, rivers, wind, etc."[4] Organic life is therefore for the child, as for the savage, "a sort of story, well regulated according to the wishes and intentions of its inventor."[5] The child is ignorant of physical law, hence uninterested in efficient causality: "Causation in the child's mind takes on the character of finalism and psychological motivation far rather than that of spatial contact."[6] Like the primitive, he does not check explanatory hypotheses by experiment[7] but instead allows his vision to be distorted by his ideas. "If he believes the sun to be alive, he will see it walking about in the sky; if he believes it to be inanimate, he will see it always motionless."[8] We need not, in view of these tendencies, be surprised that for the child "The causes of phenomena are always confused with . . . intentions."[9] His questions are of the kind asked by primitives: Why do the trees have leaves? Why does a cockchafer have antennae? Why is there lightning? A narrative explanation given by an adult satisfies him, and he turns his mind to another subject. Like the savage, he reads his own consciousness and will into the surrounding universe.

These conclusions are supported by the researches of other psychologists. Heinz Werner, in *Comparative Psychology of Mental Development*,[10] in each chapter finds similarities in the psychic habits of primitives, children, and psychotics; and Ludwig von Holzschuher, in *Praktische Psychologie: Die Primitivperson im Menschen*, asserts that "*im Kleinkind die Primitivperson geradezu allein regiert.*"[11] We are justified, I think, in assuming that discoveries about primitive thought patterns are relevant to the total psychic behavior even of

---

[4] *Language and Thought of the Child*, trans. Marjorie Gabain, New York: Meridian Books, 1955, p. 183.
[5] *Ibid.*, p. 185. [6] *Ibid.*, p. 188. [7] *Ibid.*, p. 200. [8] *Ibid.*, p. 190.
[9] *Ibid.*, p. 188. [10] Chicago: Follett Publishing Company, 1948.
[11] Seebruck am Chiemsee: Im Heering-Verlag, 1955, p. 106.

modern Westerners, not only because our sophistication falls short of making us wholly rational, but also because we were all primitives as children and carry in our mature psyches traces of childish neural patterns.

Milton's epic accordingly thrusts at us where we are racially and ontogenetically vulnerable. Its cognitive form is strangely familiar, oddly persuasive. Primitives think in this way by innate tendency, since they are neither unreflective, like beasts, nor heirs to a logical tradition of sufficient subtlety to permit the recognition that physical events result from the operation of inexorable laws. We ourselves thought in this way as children. It does not, of course, follow that we are defenseless against the poem. On the contrary, we may be stirred to vigorous resistance precisely by a feeling that we have got beyond *this* way of settling our cognitive perplexities. Nevertheless, the elementary truth that *Paradise Lost* is an enormous "tell-me-why" story, infinitely more complex than those told by children and savages but similar in basic nature, ought not to be lost sight of. No matter how richly the narrative events are overlaid and impregnated with reason, it is by the events themselves that the structure of the known universe has been determined. Rationalization explains, interprets, and justifies but stands at a farther remove from causality than the happenings.

The conclusion that *Paradise Lost* is myth is not vitiated by the poet's own realization that Christian doctrine is in part "accommodated" truth. "To know God as he really is, far transcends the powers of man's thoughts, much more of his perception," wrote Milton in a familiar passage of *The Christian Doctrine* (I, ii). We ought, he adds, "to entertain such a conception of him, as he, in condescending to accommodate himself to our capacities, has shown that he desires we should conceive." Undoubtedly God is a spirit, but if God says that He begot in Adam "a son in his own likeness, after his image," and thus attributes to Himself the physical form of a man, "why should we be afraid of attributing to him what he attributes to himself, so long as what is imperfection and weakness when viewed in reference to ourselves be considered as most complete and excellent when imputed to God?"[12] The awareness shown here that not all the statements in the Bible are literally true is reflected most clearly in the epic description of the War in Heaven. "How," asks Raphael, "shall I relate/ To human sense th' invisible exploits/ Of warring Spirits?" (v, 564-66); when his narrative is complete, he reminds Adam that in telling the story he has been "measuring things in Heav'n by things on Earth" (vi, 893). Other events in the poem, including probably whatever has no direct Biblical source—Eve's account of her dream, Raphael's visit, the quarrel of the Parents on the fatal morning, and much else—are best regarded as conscious invention, not reliable history. In such passages Milton must have hoped, at worst, not to violate either spiritual truth or fictive probability. At best, he could aspire to discover fictive metaphors which would clarify man's situation and his duties as these were implied by the Biblical story. Yet the inclusion of incidents recognized to be only metaphorically true does not weaken the epic's mythical substratum. The "true" history has been developed, embroidered, and explicated, but it continues to furnish the basic pattern.

In our century orthodox theologians have begun to speak of *Genesis* with bolder skepticism. The Biblical story of man's creation and fall, they imply, is mythical precisely as Greek and Roman stories about the gods were mythical, in that it is factually untrue. At the same time, it merits belief because, as God's metaphor, it reflects the unknowable reality accurately enough that inferences drawn from it will be trust-

---

[12] Also *Christian Doctrine*, I, ii. I use, of course, the standard translation by Bishop Charles Sumner.

worthy. C. S. Lewis has been an especially eloquent advocate of this view.[13] The source of the opinion can be found, at least partly, in discoveries about the slow emergence of the human race from lower forms of life. Few educated Christians now believe in the instantaneous creation of a first man and first woman; hence it has been necessary to subtilize the story given in *Genesis* in order to save it.

The opinion just described was certainly not Milton's. His doctrine of accommodation stopped far short of denying that an aboriginal Adam and an aboriginal Eve ate a forbidden fruit whose mortal taste brought death into the world. Yet Milton's view and Lewis's alike involve the basing of moral and religious attitudes on the events of a divine drama. The difference is that Milton would have been shocked to hear *Paradise Lost* called mythical. From one angle of vision, the distinction is significant, for it marks the transition from an older intellectual climate to a modern one. At the moment, however, I am concerned only to establish that in Milton's poem, as in hundreds of mythical cosmogonies drawn from widely varied cultures, the universe comes together less as atemporal law than as divine story. When so much has been said, it becomes evident that the poem can be illuminated not only by examining it in its own intellectual milieu and by projecting its ideas forward into our own time, but also by tracing their parallels in less sophisticated thought.

A simple illustration of the kinship between *Paradise Lost* and earlier cosmogonic myths will be helpful. Here is an excerpt from a work of scientific popularization published in 1929.

[13] For example, in *The Pilgrim's Regress*, when John, while undergoing an experience symbolic of Christian baptism, hears the voice of Wisdom saying "that all his adventures were but figurative," another voice which speaks from behind him says, "Child, if you will, it *is* mythology. It is but truth, not fact: an image, not the very real. But then it is My mythology. The words of Wisdom are also myth and metaphor. . . . But this is My inventing, this is the veil under which I have chosen to appear even from the first until now." London: Geoffrey Bles, 1946, pp. 170-71.

THE BEGINNINGS OF THE UNIVERSE

As we go forwards in time, material weight continually changes into radiation. Conversely, as we go backwards in time, the total material weight of the universe must continually increase. We have seen how the present weights of the stars are incompatible with their having existed for more than some 5 or 10 million million years, and that they would need approximately the whole of this enormous period to acquire certain signs of age which their present arrangement and motions reveal.

We have seen that the break-up of the huge extra-galactic nebulae must result in the birth of stars, and have found that the most consistent account of the origin of the galactic system of stars is provided by the supposition that the whole system originated out of the break-up of a single huge nebula some 5 to 10 million million years ago.

Let us pause for a moment to compare this with an alternative hypothesis, which some astronomers have favoured, that stars are being created all the time . . .[14]

In detail, these speculations may now be out of date. In method and tone, they are not. It is with such coolness, such impersonality, and on the basis of a similar faith in natural law that educated men tend nowadays to think about ultimate beginnings.

The tone and method of Hesiod's *Theogony*, written perhaps in the eighth century B.C., are sharply different.

First of all, the Void came into being, next broad-bosomed Earth, the solid and eternal home of all, and Eros [Desire], the most beautiful of the immortal gods, who in every man and every god softens the sinews and overpowers the prudent purpose of the mind. Out of Void came Darkness and black Night, and out of Night came Light and Day, her

[14] Sir James Jeans, *The Universe Around Us*, New York: The Macmillan Company, 1929, pp. 312-13.

9

children conceived after union in love with Darkness. Earth first produced starry Sky, equal in size with herself, to cover her on all sides. Next she produced the tall mountains, the pleasant haunts of the gods, and also gave birth to the barren waters, sea with its raging surges—all this without the passion of love. Thereafter she lay with Sky and gave birth to Ocean with its deep current, Coeus and Crius and Hyperion and Iapetus; Thea and Rhea and Themis [Law] and Mnemosyne [Memory]; also golden-crowned Phoebe and lovely Tethys.[15]

The cognitive difference between this explanation and Jeans' is enormous.

In Jeans everything is cool, logical, tentative. The grounds of the inferences are given, the nature of the reasoning process is indicated, an alternative hypothesis is offered; and nowhere are cosmological purposes hinted. Hesiod, in contrast, speaks of Night as bearing offspring after a love-union with Darkness, and of Earth, after producing Sky, Mountains, and Sea from her own resources, as lying with Sky and giving birth to Ocean and other children. Eros, or Desire, is imagined to have come into existence very early so that he might inspire generative embraces. It would be a mistake to imagine all this as purely figurative, metaphorical. "Hesiod," remarks Norman O. Brown in his introduction to the translation I have used, "lived in an age innocent of philosophy."[16] The rationalizing of cosmogony was to come later. At this stage, myth was not yet subject matter for hardheaded criticism.

Let us put side by side with these two very different passages an excerpt from Milton.

Let ther be Light, said God, and forthwith Light
Ethereal, first of things, quintessence pure

[15] *Hesiod's Theogony*, trans. Norman O. Brown, New York: The Liberal Arts Press, 1953, pp. 56-57.
[16] *Ibid.*, p. 15.

Sprung from the Deep, and from her Native East
To journie through the airie gloom began,
Spheard in a radiant Cloud, for yet the Sun
Was not; shee in a cloudie Tabernacle
Sojournd the while. God saw the Light was good;
And light from darkness by the Hemisphere
Divided: Light the Day, and Darkness Night
He nam'd. Thus was the First Day Eev'n and Morn:
Nor passd uncelebrated, nor unsung
By the Celestial Quires, when Orient Light
Exhaling first from Darkness they beheld;
Birth-day of Heav'n and Earth; with joy and shout
The hollow Universal Orb they filld,
And touchd thir Gold'n Harps, and hymning prais'd
God and his works, Creatour him they sung,
Both when first Eevning was, and when first Morn.

(VII, 243-60)

Although the quality of mind shown in Milton's description differs from that shown in the *Theogony*, a basic affinity with Hesiod is apparent. Creation results not from the pressure of physical law but from divine intention. Light is at least half a person; she springs from the deep, journeys from her native east, sojourns in a cloudy tabernacle; and watching angels hail her emergence with joy. We have come some distance toward Jeans but are still much nearer to Hesiod.

Milton's poem, then, is myth, though myth which is no longer naïve. The poet lived at a time when it was not merely possible, but necessary, to view human history as played against a background of divine will. God had made the universe, had a plan for it, and had arranged matters so that the actions of primal Man had determined the circumstances of all subsequent human experience. To be sure, the beginnings of modern science are clearly discernible in the period; but Newton had not yet shown that the positions of the planets and stars are determined by attraction. For another century, at least, "atheistic" science was to be virtually helpless against the presumption that the universe had been created for a purpose. To this intellectual situation we owe *Paradise Lost*, a poem written by a superbly cultured genius at a moment when intellectual acuity could play over and make rationally acceptable a dramatistic world view taken on faith. It was a fortunate conjunction of time, subject, and man. Today, when the metaphorical basis even of scientific thought is coming to be recognized, it begins to seem possible that serious reflection may again veer toward the formulating of "true" meanings in patterns recognized to be at least partly fictitious.

We may, however, go further. Besides being myth, and therefore having a general resemblance to myths of other times and places, *Paradise Lost* shares a mythical pattern which is so widely diffused as to give some plausibility to the claim that it is an *Urform* of human consciousness.

In a recent article in *Daedalus*, Clyde Kluckhohn, a distinguished anthropologist, remarked that "there are detectable trends toward regularities both in myths and in mythmaking." Most anthropologists, he continues, "would agree with Lévi-Strauss that throughout the world myths resemble one another to an extraordinary degree; there is, indeed, an 'astounding similarity between myths collected in different regions.'" The reason may be that "the interaction of a certain kind of biological apparatus in a certain kind of physical world with some inevitables of the human condition (the helplessness of infants, two parents of different sex, etc.) bring about some regularities in the formation of imaginative productions, of powerful images."[17] Anyone who has read widely in the mythologies of primitive peoples must have been struck by such regularities. Joseph Campbell noted them when he asserted

[17] Kluckhohn, *Daedalus*, Vol. 88 (Spring 1959), 278.

that "the new perspectives that have been opened in the fields of comparative symbolism, religion, mythology, and philosophy by the scholarship of recent years" have produced "a new image of the fundamental unity of the spiritual history of mankind."[18] Yet *Paradise Lost* appears not to have been set in this wider context except by Maude Bodkin, in a work based on Jungian assumptions; nor have I been able to discover that explicit evaluative inferences have been drawn from the conformity of Milton's immense "Tell-Me-Why" story to psychic patterns apparently implicit in man's biological nature as that is influenced by the invariables in his situation.

The choice of a way to demonstrate the conformity is perplexing. Persons who are well read in comparative mythology will need no demonstration; others will require a great deal. The simplest procedure would be to invite attention to such easily accessible collections of myths as Sir James George Frazer's *The Golden Bough*, Andrew Lang's *Myth, Ritual and Religion*, and the more recent (and still, in fact, incomplete) collection by Joseph Campbell, entitled *The Masks of God*. From these a transition can be made easily by readers whose interest has been aroused to the reports of anthropological field workers and to such theoretical discussions as those by Ernst Cassirer and Claude Lévi-Strauss. It will quickly become apparent that the resemblances are not confined to general pattern or to the invariable assumption, noted by Campbell, that there occurred in the remote past "an event, the 'mythological event' *par excellence*, which brought to an end [a] timeless way of being and effected a transformation of all things."[19] The parallels are more specific: again and again, in comparative mythology, one encounters the images

---

[18] Campbell, "The Historical Development of Mythology," *ibid.*, p. 233. This number of *Daedalus* contains a useful symposium.

[19] Campbell, *The Masks of God*, I, New York: The Viking Press, 1959, 182.

of the Father-Maker, the androgynous parent, the derivative woman become Earth-Mother, the garden of idyllic delights, the theft of a forbidden boon, a resultant calamity, and a World Tree of peculiar power. If environmental and cultural differences result in different formulations and combinations of the motifs, the resemblances are nonetheless striking. Although I dare not undertake a survey here, a very few hints of the sort of results such an investigation would turn up may be useful.

We may begin with the image of Paradise, which has a quasi-universal distribution. Students of Milton will remember the equating of Milton's Paradise by Paul Elmer More with the Hesperian Gardens of Homer, Hesiod's Golden Age, the Celtic Tir-nan-og, the Arcadia of the pastoral poets and of Sidney, the Forest of Arden, the Land of the Living Heart, Tennyson's island valley of Avilion, and all the other Utopias to be found in ancient myth and modern literature. "Turn where you will," he wrote, "and you will find this pastoral ideal haunting the imagination of men. . . . Were one to attempt to display its universality by illustration, one would need to abridge the libraries of the world into a few pages."[20] To More's citations one could add endlessly; for example (since I emphasized the accessibility of the childish mind to mythological patterns), Frances Hodgson Burnett's *The Secret Garden*, which has strongly impressed many young imaginations. In the present context, however, I must stress not literary parallels but mythological. "We encounter the 'paradise myth' all over the world," says Mircea Eliade, "in more or less complex forms. . . . All these myths show primitive man enjoying blessedness, spontaneity, and liberty, which he has most annoyingly lost as the consequence of the 'fall,' that is, as the

[20] Paul Elmer More, "The Theme of *Paradise Lost*," in *Shelburne Essays*, Fourth Series, New York: G. P. Putnam's Sons, 1907, p. 224.

result of a mythical occurrence which has brought about the rupture between Heaven and Earth."[21] The notion carries with it many subsidiary images common to Milton's poem and the primitive analogues: of mild weather, friendship between man and animals, food obtainable without exertion, and easier commerce than has since been possible between man and the gods. Here is the narrative core of *Paradise Lost*, so widely and richly paralleled that John M. Patrick has recently speculated—venturesomely, I fear—whether primordial man did not preserve across the millennia dim memories of a paradise he did in fact enjoy before the coming of four successive ice ages drove him to a difficult and perilous existence on the edge of glaciers.[22]

This fall, found everywhere in mythology, is regularly the effect of some transgression. For instance, among the Andaman Islanders, a Negrito people isolated for centuries in the Bay of Bengal, it resulted from the breaking of a taboo against the making of noise while cicadas are singing. We may follow this version briefly in order to observe how much of Milton's story is present in an almost certainly unrelated myth in which the incidents are adapted to a different cultural milieu and arranged in a different order. As a result of the violation, say the Andamanese, "a great storm came and killed many people, who were turned into fishes and birds."[23] The human survivors were dispersed, each pair being provided with a different dialect.[24] Although reported versions of the myth vary slightly, we seem to have here an amalgam

[21] "The Yearning for Paradise in Primitive Tradition," *Daedalus*, Vol. 88 (Spring 1959), 255-56.

[22] John M. Patrick, *Milton's Conception of Sin as Developed in Paradise Lost*, Logan, Utah: Utah State University Press Monograph Series, Vol. 7 (June 1960), 7-9.

[23] A. R. Brown, *The Andaman Islanders: A Study in Social Anthropology*, Cambridge, Mass.: University Press, 1922, p. 206.

[24] I follow the suggestions of M. V. Portman and E. H. Man, cited *ibid.*, pp. 212-13.

of three separate incidents in the Christian story—the fall, the deluge, and the building of Babel. In both narratives, however, explanations are offered of important aspects of the essential human situation. We do not live in a Paradise; men are divided into culturally distinct groups; and the forms of human speech vary. Elsewhere the fall is imaged otherwise, but it is often present in some form as the cause of a disparity between the actual conditions of life and those better ones men are capable of envisaging.

A few additional parallels must be lumped together in a paragraph. At the beginning there was usually a dark chaos; it was so in ancient India,[25] among the ancient Babylonians,[26] and among the Jicarilla Apaches.[27] The Creator God, who may double as Adam, very often produces living creatures from his own body, as Milton's Adam produced Eve from his rib. (Apparently the search for ultimate origins forces the mind back to unity.) The Sanskrit *Brahmanas* say that Purusha produced a husband and wife by dividing himself;[28] the Polynesian Vari-ma-te-takere "plucked off a bit of her *right* side, and it became a human being";[29] in the Icelandic *Edda* we read of Ymir, who begot a man and a woman from his left hand.[30] Again, the first human beings are sometimes made from earth, as God made Adam—earth, because of its plasticity and also because primitive man feels deeply his own continuity with nature, being a suitable material. This happened among the Salishan tribes of America,[31] among the Alabama

[25] Cf. Andrew Lang, *Myth, Ritual and Religion*, i, London: Longmans, Green and Co., 1913, 232.

[26] Cf. Joseph Campbell, *The Hero with a Thousand Faces*, New York: Meridian Books, 1956, p. 284.

[27] Morris Edward Opler, *Myths and Tales of the Jicarilla Apache Indians*, New York: American Folk-Lore Society, 1938, p. 1.

[28] Lang, *Myth, Ritual and Religion*, i, 239.

[29] Gill, *Myths and Songs*, p. 3.

[30] Campbell, *Masks of God*, i, 107.

[31] Franz Boas, ed., *Folk-Tales of Salishan and Sahaptin Tribes*, Lancaster, Pa.: The American Folk-Lore Society, 1917, p. 84.

Indians,[32] and among the Dahomean Negroes of Africa.[33] The mother produced in this way, or by division from aboriginal man, often becomes the ancestress of the human race. Finally, the importance of an aboriginal tree of some kind is frequently very great. Campbell has collected a series of examples in *The Masks of God*,[34] and I have myself discovered others. Although the Christian use of the tree as the source of a forbidden fruit, and later as the cross on which Christ redeemed the world, is special, the notion of a World Tree as a source of vital energy and as a link between the lower and upper worlds appears often. Still other parallels have to do with the long life of first men, their ability to converse with animals—as Eve conversed with the serpent—and the coming of Death into the world; but these I have space barely to mention.

Up to this point I have been trying to say two things. First, in basic character *Paradise Lost* is "primitive," not in being simpleminded but in sharing much of the content and shape of cosmogonic stories found in ancient records and still current among undeveloped peoples, and also in resolving cognitive wonder about the origin of the human situation by telling a story, exactly as savages have done in all ages and as children still try to do. Secondly, the events described in *Paradise Lost* are remarkably similar to those in other cosmogonic myths, so that we may suspect a fitness in the mythic incidents to satisfy psychological needs.

The second point must be developed a little further. The image of Paradise appeals to us, I suggest, because the stresses of living often make us yearn for restful ease. The image of the arch rebel invigorates us because we have all had to

[32] John R. Swanton, *Myths and Tales of the Southeastern Indians*, Washington, D.C.: Bureau of American Ethnology, Bulletin 88, 1929, p. 118.

[33] Melville J. and Frances S. Herskovits, *Dahomean Narrative: A Cross-Cultural Analysis*, Evanston, Ill.: Northwestern University Press, 1958, p. 151.

[34] Campbell, *Masks of God*, I, 106-107 and 119-21.

inhibit aggressive urges and enjoy seeing them indulged by personages with whom we can empathize. The image of the mother-wife moves us because the strong emotional tie to the mother is rarely completely broken and the sexual drives makes the contemplation of an attractive woman pleasurable. The punishment of the arch rebel gratifies us exactly as a child is gratified by earned punishment: suffering "wipes out" the transgression and reintegrates the transgressor with the social group. The promise that Paradise will ultimately be restored, if our behavior merits the favor, at once justifies the communal *mores* and promises us a reward adequate to compensate for the continued inhibiting of forbidden impulses.

A possibility has been raised by certain biological experiments that there may be an organic predisposition to respond to special images. Young ducks shrink if a model of a hawk is drawn over their cage, but not if the model is that of a gull, a duck, a heron, or a pigeon, and not if the model of the hawk is reversed, so that the long tail precedes the short neck.[35] Other experiments show that the grayling butterfly has so strong an inherited preference for a dark hue in females of its species that it is more excited by a very dark model than by the darkest living female, and that a human child between the ages of three and six months will smile at the appearance either of a human face or of a model of the face, but at nothing else.[36] Apparently, as Adolf Portmann, a Swiss biologist, remarks, "behavior patterns which relate to environmental circumstances that have still to be encountered can be prepared in the nervous and sensory organization of animals. Structures lie ready which permit the recognition of what has never before been perceived."[37] Although we have all been aware that instinctive drives are transmitted geneti-

[35] See Adolf Portmann, *Das Problem der Urbilder in Biologischer Sicht*, *Eranos Jahrbuch*, Vol. 18, Zürich: Rhein-Verlag, 1950, 422.

[36] Campbell, *Masks of God*, I, 43 and 46.

[37] Portmann, *Problem der Urbilder*, p. 422.

cally, the discovery that certain forms and colors can trigger behavior mechanisms, whereas other very similar ones do not, may come as a surprise.

From such findings it is, of course, a long and perilous jump to the conclusion that the root images of *Paradise Lost* are "innate releasing mechanisms" (to adopt Joseph Campbell's phrase) for strongly affective reactions in mature human beings. We must limit ourselves to the observation that, whether learned or inherited, reactions to the images have appeared in innumerable societies from remote antiquity to the present. My own guess would be that certain objects and situations are structurally similar to states of consciousness—either static or dynamic—induced by inevitable human experiences. From this point of view, the real subject matter of *Paradise Lost*, on the nontheological and nonphilosophical level, would be the sense of loss, accompanied by a conviction of personal responsibility, felt when blissful immaturity is exchanged for responsible but self-distrustful adulthood. The resonance of the mythic events would thus be explained as deriving from their embodiment of a traumatic experience lived through not only by the race but also by every normal individual in it.

A final problem must now be faced. Does not what I have been saying apply equally to other Christian poems in the Celestial Cycle, including the most inept? Have I not, in fact, been speaking rather of Christianity than of Milton? Or why only of Christianity? If my reasoning has been correct, ought not we to be strongly moved by any story which includes a Father-Maker, a Paradise, an Original Transgression, and the rest of the usual incidents? What, in a word, is special about Milton's epic? The question has not yet been answered even indirectly and deserves the best reply I can give.

First, I assert emphatically that the monomyth described earlier does have, potentially, an intrinsic power. More's essay, from which I have quoted, is one testimony of that power; and his examples are not all Christian. On the other hand, not all tellings of the myth impress sophisticated Westerners; and, of all the Christian versions, only Dante's *Commedia*, which is not about the loss of Paradise, has the critical repute of *Paradise Lost*. How, then, does Milton succeed in making the events of his story unusually impressive, so that they are given an opportunity to work upon our subrational sensitivities?

A very important part of the total answer is of course that Milton's style is superior to those of his rivals. When Sylvester writes (*Devine Weekes*, Second Week, Day I, Part II), "Lord (answeres *Eue*), the Serpent did intice/ My simple frailty to this sinfull vice," we are not overwhelmed. In this dress, the myth finds us impervious to its charms; and stylistic analysis would partly reveal why. Something more than style is involved, however. *What* Milton says is more powerful than what Sylvester says, besides being said more skillfully. I propose to leave the stylistic superiority to one side, as not requiring demonstration, in order to comment on matter; but I wish to urge, in passing, that style depends not only on resounding or glittering words and deft measures but also on what is admitted into the work as image and idea and what is kept out.

The burden of my first comment will be that the myth is not quickly repudiated as we read Milton because we become aware that the events are being filtered to us through a mind which, if its modes of operation may seem archaic, nevertheless clearly has a native critical capacity fully the equal of our own. (For the moment I am thinking of readers who do not rebel violently. Something will be said later about those who do.) T. S. Eliot has said that he can accept Dante's worldview while reading the *Divina Commedia* because he can recognize its intelligence and self-consistency; despite Mr. Eliot's differing reaction to Milton, a similar principle applies here. We are told not only how the events occurred, as is usual, but, in persuasive detail, why. The happenings are not arbitrary but reasoned, justified. This we do not get, in anything like the same degree, in Sylvester or any other English poet of the tradition. The ordinary tendency is not so much to rationalize as to decorate, to embroider, to catalogue, to exclaim. The rhetorical virtue most sought after is "invention," which may go so far as to deflect notice from the substantial myth to its trappings. Milton invents, too, as in Books V-VII. For the most part, however, he keeps the simple mythical framework central and uses his enormous intellectual energy to make it acceptable. His reward is the activation of both parts of the reader's mind, the cortex by thought, the primitive residue by the mythic events. The cognitive density of the poem thus helps (unless it hinders, as we shall observe shortly) to reconcile us to its mythic content, which is freed to purvey the subrational satisfactions of which I have spoken.

In what has just been said I have not been thinking merely of the straightforwardly philosophical passages, like those in Books III, VIII, XI, and XII. These are important for the rational intelligence and could not be spared; they conquer scruples and help us to give qualified acceptance to the Divine Plan. Yet what I have called the pressure of intellect makes itself felt everywhere in a pervasive tone of massive good sense. The poem is steadily weighty, not weighty only here and there—as, in a different way, is Dante's *Commedia*. In reading it we are regularly in contact not only with a sensitivity but also with an intelligence, as we are not when we read savage myths or even when we dip into other poems of the Celestial Cycle.

Secondly, while all this is going on, something else is happening. The impressive rationality of the poem of course helps us to take the myth seriously—as is demonstrated by the tendency of unsympathetic critics to find fault with Milton's handling of it. We do not bother to point out flaws in the cosmogonic myths of the Dahomean Negroes or the Andaman Islanders, or even to quarrel with Sylvester about theology. But there is also a more indirect effect of the poem's strong appeal to reason. It is not true, I think, that the reason works best when the subconscious mind is quiescent, any more than it is true that the aesthetic imagination works most effectively when the rational powers are suspended. Mental work is often done most efficiently when total awareness is heightened. My own experience, at least, is that stimulation spreads gradually from one kind of psychic activity to another. Accordingly, while the reason is strongly engaged by Milton's learning and good sense, the nondiscursive sensitivities are quickened by a sort of contagion and the mythical images are given an unusual opportunity to gain a leverage on the feelings. If we are fully caught up in the poem, totally absorbed by it (as happens for some readers at some times), we respond, on the subconscious level, by enjoying Satan's indulgence of aggressive impulses, luxuriating in the innocent sensuality of the primeval Garden, recognizing in Eve both the yearned-for mother and the sweetly intoxicating mate (or in Adam both the father and the husband), and finally, as the epic slopes to its conclusion, acquiescing in the vicarious punishments which reintegrate us with the oppressive social group. The condition of this two-sided experience is precisely the vigorous stimulation of both discursive and nondiscursive mentality which we get in Dante and Milton but not in lesser poets. If the reason were not kept actively at work inside the poem, under the poem's conditions, it would be released to criticize the mythical images less sympathetically from a distance; but the infection of each half of the mind by the excitement of the other half also plays an important role.

Unfortunately, perhaps, the analysis can be reversed. For

some readers, Milton's method does not work. The combination of hard reasoning and myth is for such persons exactly wrong; they can take myth or reasoning separately, but not both together. The reason for this inability deserves brief consideration.

For a few people the explanation may be that their minds are capable of only one kind of intense activity at a time. It has been argued that the dialogue in films should lack literary distinction because the viewer's eyes are bombarded with visual images which necessarily distract his attention from words. I do not myself find much weight in the objection. In Sir Laurence Olivier's film of *Henry V*, for example, the richness of the settings appeared to me to reinforce the poetry, not to weaken it; everything (I should say) depends on the fitness of the images to the words. Yet the criticism has been repeated so often that it may well reflect the experience of some viewers. If so, the *Gesamtkunstwerk* of whatever kind may make an especially powerful impact on some minds while merely confusing others. Something analogous may be true of other mixtures. I am acquainted with readers who believe that the introduction of a homely illustration into serious discourse breaks tonality, whereas other readers are pleased to see meaning opening into an additional dimension. The combining of myth with hard reasoning, however, appears to raise an exceptionally complicated problem.

One of its aspects may have to do with a tendency for the mythopoeic and discursive faculties to lie in separate mental areas, so that commerce between them is painful. We have all, perhaps, known people who are infuriated by attempts to "interpret" dreams. When the subject matter of a poem is the basic substance of Christianity itself, fear may sometimes be awakened lest rational criticism result in the weakening of faith. More frequently, however, the difficulty may be of an opposite kind: a part of Milton's modern audience is pulled in a direction in which it senses psychic danger to lie. The reader whose hold on rationality is infirm—for example, the deconverted Christian who is determined not to be swayed into acceptance of a renounced faith—feels threatened and protects himself by developing aversion. I think the aversion would not be so strong, as it sometimes evidently is, if the threat were not great; and the reasons why it is great may be partly those I have tried to explain.

Of course other forces are often at work, too. For instance, undisciplined minds may not be up to the job of following Milton's syntax, with the result that attention wanders and reading becomes disagreeable. The resistance I have especially in mind, however, is that of perceptive and capable readers who can enjoy such difficult authors as Donne or Joyce or James but feel for *Paradise Lost* a repugnance amounting almost to hatred. The emotion cannot always be the result of convictions about poetic style, for it sometimes appears in bright students whose critical ideas are still unformed. On the principle that the faults we detest most in others are those to which we feel ourselves peculiarly liable, it seems to me not improbable that Milton's epic works on the subconscious minds of unfit readers so energetically that the conscious mind is forced to cast about for weapons of defense.

No matter which way it operates, the double-facedness I have attempted to describe is, I suggest, a major source of the power felt in *Paradise Lost* by readers who, despite rational sophistication, have retained contact with the preliterate forms of childish and primitive mentality. Only such readers, perhaps, are capable of sensing the poem's extraordinary range; and among them, the sense is almost certainly strongest in those who offer no indignant resistance. For them, if not for everybody—and certainly not for all college undergraduates—*Paradise Lost* releases what Campbell has called "central excitatory mechanisms"[38] and goes far toward verifying

Gerhart Hauptmann's assertion that *Dichten heisst, hinter Worten das Urwort erklingen lassen.*[39]

[38] Campbell, *Masks of God*, 1, 48.   [39] Quoted *ibid.*, p. 55.

....

CHAPTER II

THE

NARRATIVE

PLAN

Although Milton's epic is based on the Scriptures and Christian tradition, not everything in it is an essential part of Christianity. He manipulated his story, adding incidents, rearranging their order, and introducing rational explications. I would next like to examine the gross narrative structure, ignoring the rationalizations, in order to discover what additional significance can be found in the major actions. Neither, for the time being, will much attention be paid to style. It will be convenient to follow the incidents in chronological order, just as it would be convenient in summarizing the Oedipus story to begin with the prophecy that led to the child's exposure.

In the baldest possible summary the story runs more or less as follows. I have tried to avoid inserting phrases which indicate logical relationships.

God announces the exaltation of His Son. Satan conceives envy and retires into the north of Heaven with his followers. He incites the followers to revolt. Abdiel resists, and upon his return to the Holy Mount is praised. The fight which follows between the good and bad angels is a draw. The Son, at His Father's command, sweeps the rebels over the edge of Heaven. They fall through Chaos and into Hell. The Son, again by His Father's order, issues into Chaos to create Earth, the surround-

*ing universe, and man. Upon His return to Heaven, the angels
sing praise. In Hell, Satan and his followers build Pandaemonium and hold a conference. It is decided that an attempt
will be made to seek out Earth with the intention either of
destroying it and its inhabitants or of occupying it. Satan
makes his way through Chaos to Earth. God sees him, predicts
man's fall, and accepts the Son's offer to suffer punishment on
man's behalf. While engaged in a preliminary attempt to
persuade Eve to sin, Satan is discovered and ejected from
the Garden. As he secretly explores the Earth, God sends
Raphael to warn Adam of his danger. After Raphael's departure, Adam and Eve quarrel about whether to work separately or together; Eve wins, and they part. Satan returns to
the Garden as a serpent and provokes Eve to eat the forbidden
fruit. Eve persuades Adam to do the same. The Son is sent to
pronounce judgment. Satan returns to Hell to boast of his ac-
complishment and is transformed with his followers, temporarily, into a snake. In the meantime, Sin and Death come to
Earth to begin their evil work. Michael is ordered by God to
reveal to Adam the future results of his sin. At the end of
the colloquy, Adam is comforted by the promise of a Redeemer. He and Eve are ejected from the Garden.*

Obviously, this summary might be expanded or further com-
pressed, but it will serve as a basis for remarks about Milton's
large-scale plan.

Much of the story is of course Milton's invention, or was
adapted by him from extra-Biblical sources to flesh out his
narrative scheme. The basic source in *Genesis* (Chaps. I-III)
contains only some 1,800 words against Milton's 10,565 lines.
If Books XI and XII, which are drawn from other parts of
the Bible, are excluded from the calculation, the lines are de-
creased to 9,015, but the disproportion is still very great. Of
the 1,800 words in *Genesis* I-III, about 725 describe the Cre-

ation; if these, together with Milton's Book VII, which covers the same ground, are also excluded, the proportion is 1,110 words to 8,275 lines, or, at an average of 7.77 words to each of Milton's lines, 1,110 Biblical words to 64,297 in the epic. This is to say that Books I-VI and VIII-X of *Paradise Lost* expand their direct Biblical source by some fifty-eight times: a procedure dictated by the necessity that an epic poem, as a work in a diffuse genre, attain considerable size. Invention of some kind was therefore unavoidable. The only choice was between the complicating of events and the luxurious proliferation of description.

In this situation, the choice made by Du Bartas, the predecessor to whom Milton's debt seems to have been especially great, had been to describe inexhaustibly. Milton describes too—in fatiguing detail, it may appear to some readers—but he also greatly multiplied the number of events. The building of Pandaemonium, the journey of Satan through Chaos, the allegory of Sin and Death, the War in Heaven, the visits to the Garden of Raphael and Michael, the quarrel between Adam and Eve, and much else is mainly his own. Of course he accepted hints from many sources, including the Bible, theological tradition, and the classics. The War in Heaven has its basis in a few verses of *Revelation* and is elaborated in Homeric and Virgilian terms, with borrowings also from Hesiod; the voyage through Chaos assumes conventional scientific notions about the elements and their qualities; and specific sources of one kind or another can be found for most of the other details. Absolute invention seems to be nearly impossible. Nonetheless, the epic as we have it includes much that is not present in other treatments of Milton's subject. We may therefore consider the events as indicative not merely of what was implicit in the narrative of man's fall but also of the author's attitude toward his materials.

A little study of the synopsis reveals that the actions are

chiefly of three kinds. One set of events has to do with evil, one with the punishment of evil, and one with reward and comfort. Only one item refuses to fit into any of the categories—the drawn contest between the good and bad angels; and this, the poem tells us plainly, could have had no issue had not the Son joined the fray. The discovery has a certain interest because the futility of the epic battle has often been noticed. If the action is isolated, in the sense of having no parallel elsewhere in the poem, of entering into no pattern, implying no meaning which is corroborated by other actions, criticism of the incident may be just. Although a systematic approach is not necessary to call attention to the war's pointlessness, the presence on one's desk of a solitary card which refuses to be grouped with other cards suggests that the war is not successfully assimilated into the poem's structure.

Ten of the actions are, in one way or another, tainted, reprehensible. Two of these might not, under other circumstances, be evil: the building of Pandaemonium in preparation for the council and Satan's journey through Chaos. The council, however, is vitiated both by the character of the personages and by the decision at which they arrive, and the passage through Chaos takes its moral color from the revengeful purpose by which it is motivated.

The remaining eight actions in this group are unmistakably evil. The retirement of Satan into the north is inspired by envy for the Son; the inciting of armed conflict aims at the breaking of hierarchy; the decision to destroy or occupy Earth is malicious, as are the two attempts of Satan to pervert Eve's will, the first frustrated, the second prosperous; the quarrel of Adam and Eve points forward to the Fall; the seduction of Adam by Eve is the central calamity of the whole poem; and the coming to Earth of Sin and Death bodes ill for all humankind.

The argument between Adam and Eve on the fatal morning has a particular interest here because its connection with the other seven gives it an unmistakable taint. In the logical structure of the poem, Eve's insistence on working apart from her husband is clearly guiltless, if not, perhaps, quite blameless. Before the Fall, the only possible sin is that of eating the forbidden fruit. As his hierarchical inferior, Eve of course ought to have heeded Adam's warnings; she is "inferiour, in the mind/ And inward Faculties, which most excell" (VIII, 541-42), and therefore should have yielded to his advice. Yet the exercise of moral freedom is sinful only when the consequent action is bad: we are told that Eve is "yet sinless" (IX, 659) some 275 lines after she has withdrawn her hand from Adam's to depart to her solitary labor. Evidently a distinction is to be drawn between actions which are in some degree blameworthy and those which are sinful. Neither, certainly, is Adam seriously at fault in allowing Eve to claim some freedom. We remember God's assertion that there is no pleasure in forced obedience (III, 103-11), His granting of freedom to the bad angels to revolt, His gift of self-determination to Adam and Eve, and even Satan's permitting of Abdiel to return to the Holy Mount. Yet the stubborn tendency both of critics and of untutored readers to impute error at this point to the conduct of the parents reveals an instinctive recognition that the quarrel borrows its moral color from other similar revolts against hierarchy which lead up to and away from it. Like a harmless young man who falls into bad company, the dispute becomes guilty by association. If reason understands that the separation is innocent, the feelings persuade us that it is not.

A second set of actions balances and partly negates the first. The ejection of the rebel angels from Heaven, their fall through Chaos, the driving of Satan from Paradise after discovery by the angelic guard, the pronouncing of judgment by the Son, the protracted description to Adam of evils which will plague his descendants, and the removal of Adam and Eve from the Garden are reactions by the divine Power against revolt. In the mythic world every thrust is met by a counter-thrust; the sentient universe pushes back against any pressure, not mechanically, for Divine Will is constantly at work, but inevitably. As in cosmogonic stories everywhere—indeed, as in all fiction, for cosmogony has the structure of fiction—no major action is without consequence. Moreover, the direction of events is irreversible: the world will remain permanently what it is made by the ricocheting of evil gestures from Divine purpose. This again is a mythic quality of the narrative economy. The subject of the poem is events which, by virtue of happening once *in illo tempore*, at the beginning of things, have determined the nature of the world we know.

The third set of events has to do with lifting, upraising, giving reward and comfort. Of seven happenings, the first, the exaltation of the Son, fits least easily into the group when studied in context. If the exaltation is motivated by love and deserved by merit, the phrases in which it is announced are nevertheless preponderantly negative. "Your Head I him appoint . . . have sworn to him shall bow/ All knees in Heav'n . . . him who disobeyes/ Mee disobeyes . . . Cast out from God and blessed vision, falls/ Into utter darkness, deep ingulft . . ." (v, 606-14). In contrast, the action itself (a kind of coronation) is strongly positive; and the stylistic tonality is no concern to us at the moment. The remaining six events are less ambivalent. Abdiel is praised for the resistance he has offered to Satan; the creation of Earth and the surrounding universe by the Son is intended to repair the "detriment" occasioned by the loss of the rebel angels from Heaven (vii, 152-53); upon the Son's return to Heaven the loyal angels sing praises to Jehovah, who had commanded the act; when in Book III the fall of man is predicted, the Son volunteers to bear man's punishment; the sending of Raphael to warn Adam of his danger results in Adam's learning what he must know if the temptation is not to find him unprepared; and finally, at the end of Book XII, Adam is comforted by the promise of a Redeemer who will reopen a path to Heaven for sinful human beings.

The effect of these actions, as a group, is to temper with mercy the justice of earned punishment and to suggest God's quickness to reward merit. The reaction of things-as-they-are to disturbance is not merely punitive; Divine Power goes out of its way to be a little more gracious than is necessary. Even the freedom allowed the fallen angels to invade Earthly Paradise contributes to this impression. The devils do not long remain chained in Hell but are allowed to hold meetings, to formulate aggressive plans, and, after Satan's success on Earth, to exchange their doleful shades for a pleasanter habitation. Without these actions, the first and second groups of events would be roughly in balance: evil, the narrative framework would imply, does not exert itself without encountering resistance. With them, the balance is strongly tilted toward cosmic benevolence. The fact is too seldom perceived by critics who persist in believing Milton's religion to be dourly Puritanical and based predominantly on Old Testament attitudes.

In psychological terms the first of the three groups is easily recognized to derive basically from the id and the second from the superego, although not much depends on the use of these terms. The process of acculturation requires the suppressing of natural drives—the instinct to fight when angered, to run when afraid, to satisfy appetites in ways not culturally sanctioned; to act, in a word, on a purely instinctual level, as though only the well-being of the self were important. The aggressive actions of the Devil's party function, accordingly, as projections of the reader's stored-up resentments.[1] The

---

[1] For a fuller treatment of this subject, see my *Literature and the Irrational: A Study in Anthropological Backgrounds*, Englewood Cliffs, N.J.: Prentice-Hall, 1960, pp. 172-89.

spectacle of evil thrashing about violently in resistance to authority gratifies wishes which may have been thrust beneath consciousness but have not on that account ceased to exist. In childhood we all have felt momentary hatred of the parent and the teacher; in adulthood we have not always seen eye to eye with the Boss. Indeed, it is possible that Satanist critics are especially appreciative of acts symbolizing rebellion because they have had unusually frustrated early lives. But there are also in every human being moral convictions produced by a group ethos. The parent, the policeman, the judge, God, are representatives of authoritative principles whom we both fear and respect. As a child who is forced to do a task which he has resisted may afterwards feel cheerful because of his reacceptance into parental approval, so the discomfiting of evil by good reassures the part of the mind which seeks protection against a sense of guilt by acquiescence to communal mores.

The gratification of the superego is no less important to literature than the satisfying of the id, since the superego's importance in the total economy of the psyche is normally very great. One of the faults of such a work as Byron's *Cain*, in which revolt is expected to win admiration, is that the superego is not finally reassured. Although a young reader, often a bright young man at the point of development when virility is associated with unlimited self-assertion, may be enormously excited by *Cain*, mature persons feel that the drama lacks a satisfying resolution. The overweighting of rebellion implies that the work must be completed by the carrying over of the recommended attitudes into extraliterary experience. But one of the comparatively few conclusions on which modern aesthetics appears to have settled is that art must have an apparent self-sufficiency; that the aesthetic universe, although it may reflect the "real" universe with considerable accuracy, ought not finally to conduct the percipient into ordinary life through a gap in its perimeter. Resolution must be attained inside the work's limits; whatever tensions are provoked must be released within the virtual world of the art object, not outside it. Thus in spite of the tendency of artists to be social nonconformists, literature is fundamentally conservative. The aesthetic status of works that stimulate social reform—Upton Sinclair's *The Jungle*, Harriet Beecher Stowe's *Uncle Tom's Cabin*, Gerhart Hauptmann's *Die Weber*—is regularly questionable.

Milton might have become a champion of revolutionary views in ethics or psychology as well as in politics and theology. He comes, indeed, so near to being a Satanist that the Satanist view of *Paradise Lost*, if not finally tenable, is easily understood. Again and again the lines reverberate with antiauthoritarian passion. "Fall'n Cherube, to be weak is miserable" (i, 157); "courage never to submit or yeild" (i, 108); "The mind is its own place, and in it self/ Can make a Heav'n of Hell, a Hell of Heav'n" (i, 254-55): the appropriate response to these speeches, and to other similar ones, is exhilarated assent. The long speech of Belial at the great consult in Hell is an even more striking illustration that Milton's acceptance of cosmic authority was precarious. Belial's speech is not only the most temperate of all those delivered in Pandaemonium, it is also the wisest. Only a hint of sincere repentance is needed to make it objectively right in the poem's own terms. If we adjust to our new circumstances and cease to offend God, Belial argues, our punishment may gradually be lightened. Short of advising actual repentance—which he could not have done without ceasing to be a devil—Belial could have offered no sounder proposal. Yet the judgment of his speech by the epic narrator is uncompromisingly negative: "Thus *Belial* with words cloath'd in reasons garb/ Counseld ignoble ease, and peaceful sloath" (ii, 226-27). Especially in Books I and II, *Paradise Lost* trembles on the verge of precisely the kind of spiritual intransigence which leads rather to inflammatory protest than to art.

As a whole, the epic is not intransigent. The divine reactions to evil imply that in the moral world, as in the physical one, every force generates an opposite force. To be sure, good does not obliterate evil by responding to it any more than the northward leap of a boat from which a diver has sprung southward returns the diver to the boat and the boat to its former position; but the universe responds to moral shocks exactly as it does to physical. If the rebel shakes his fist at the God-Parent-Teacher-Policeman image, he cannot expect the gesture to go unnoticed.

The demonstration, in the third group of incidents, that God's reactions are not meanly punitive but benevolent and gracious carries reconciliation to things-as-they-are even furthur. Adam's final understanding of God's plan provokes an exclamation whose importance has been taught us by Professor Lovejoy.

> O goodness infinite, goodness immense!
> That all this good of evil shall produce,
> And evil turn to good!
>
> (XII, 469-71)

Far from simply meeting pressure with counterpressure, God adds voluntary mercies. The Son was not required, except by His own loving nature, to bear the greater part of man's punishment for sin. The dispatching of Raphael to warn Adam of coming danger, and of Michael to assure Adam that all is not finally lost although the consequences of sin will be terrible, is a supererogatory addition to the requirements of justice. Neither does God spare praise when it has been earned—by Abdiel, by the Son, by Adam himself before the Fall. True, Milton lived in a period when under normal conditions monarchy was thought to be the natural form of government, and he portrayed God as a very grand king, not as an irresponsible grandfather whose fondness is expressed by hugs and the distribution of toys. Milton's deity cannot be cuddled up to but must be adored as infinitely superior to His creatures. He is presentimental, pre-Romantic, prehumanitarian; and His love, like Christian charity, is characterized not by emotional turbulence but by a settled and persistent good will. Nevertheless, benevolence is implicit in the texture of incidents, if not in a melting softness of the Divine character, and must be recognized by a sound criticism.

The total structure meets its severest test at the beginning of Book III, when whatever sympathies have been created for Satan are to be firmly and permanently suppressed. The scene shifts to Heaven, where God, surrounded by all His angels, is to place Satan's mission to earth in cosmic perspective. Much depends on success here, for failure will cause the entire remainder of the poem to be skewed. To judge from much recent criticism, the effort did not come off well. Let us inquire what judgment is suggested by the incidents themselves dissociated, insofar as they can be dissociated, from the style.

For several reasons, the view of Satan flying toward the world ought not to be intrinsically gratifying to the reader. The invocation to Book III, which is separate from the narrative plot, nonetheless is full of signals which tell us that Heaven, as a place of light, is infinitely preferable to Hell, a place of darkness. More important, the favorable opinion which may have been induced by Satan's intrepid speeches has already been considerably modified by distaste for the malicious errand upon which he is bent. We have learned that the "happy seat/ Of som new Race calld *Man*" is to be wasted or possessed by the devils as their own. The "punie habitants" are either to be driven out or seduced to the devils' party, "that thir God/ May prove thir foe, and with repenting hand/ Abolish his own works." Success in the enterprise, we have been told, "would surpass/ Common revenge," for God would be saddened by it and the devils made joyful.[2] If all this thrashing about for the purpose of resisting authority has given momentary pleasure to the antisocial part of the reader's mind, it has also left a bad taste behind. The healthy psyche is not wholly delighted by the destruction of innocent happiness, especially when the agent is a cynical bully whose real animus is against somebody other than his victim. Releasing pent-up inhibitions is one thing; planning a sneaky attack on your enemy's small son, as he plays harmlessly in the patio, is another. But there is still a third force which helps our sympathies to swing at this point to the other side.

That force is generated by a shift in the point of view. Up to this moment, we have been seeing things as the devils saw them, feeling the devils' smart, sharing their sense of frustration. Now we find ourselves looking at evil from the outside; and its appearance changes remarkably. God "foretells the success of *Satan* in perverting Mankind; clears his own Justice and Wisdom from all imputation, having created Man free and able anough to have withstood his Tempter." Unless something has gone wrong with the style (which is not presently our concern), or the reasoning in God's speech is patently absurd (but rationality, again, is not what we are presently examining), we will accept the condemnation of Satan's enterprise because we share for the time being the state of mind from which it issues.

The almost irresistible power of the writer to manipulate his reader's attitudes by shifting the point of view has not, I think, been sufficiently emphasized by criticism. For example, in a novel about the relations between labor and management, a skillful writer can make the typical reader sympathize, at least for the duration of the fictive spell, with members of the union, with their somewhat unscrupulous

2 See *Paradise Lost*, II, 347-73.

leaders, with management, with a Congressional committee engaged in the exposure of racketeers, with police officers responsible for the maintenance of order, or with all these in turn. His method consists, roughly, of opening the reader's consciousness to data as they appear to an actor with a special emotional bias. Comparatively few people are conscious hypocrites. Most of them contrive by an instinct of self-protection to believe sincerely that, under the circumstances, their opinions are right and their actions justified. Let the novelist admit us to the mind of a corrupt labor leader who has suffered terribly from capitalist oppression, and he will succeed, if his imagination works effectively, in making us sense the leader's machinations as he himself senses them. One of the values of literature is that it can increase wonderfully our recognition of the complexities in experience by showing us life as it appears to people whose characters and backgrounds differ markedly from our own.

To be sure, the cutting edge of the technique can be turned the other way, so that the consciousness we are made to enter becomes repugnant. Shakespeare's Iago, his Richard III, his Edmund, in their soliloquies and other speeches show their wills to be unscrupulous and selfish. Empathizing with them is difficult because a malice of which we would not admit ourselves to be guilty is exposed nakedly. Again, J. P. Marquand makes the narrator of *The Late George Apley* despicable by causing him to reveal, very gradually, an astonishing insensitivity to the data he records. Only what flatters his prejudices *tells* for him; the reader is encouraged to draw different inferences. As a rule, however, we assume, at least initially, the reliability of what we perceive from a limited angle of vision, and we expect deceptions to be signaled to us. Where they are not signaled, as in Agatha Christie's *The Murder of Roger Ackroyd*, whatever admiration we may feel for the author's dexterity is complicated by an outraged awareness that we have been cheated. *The Murder of Roger Ack-royd* shocks because the first-person narrator, who turns out to have been the criminal, has not given himself away and consequently is the sole character whose guilt is unthinkable.

Now Satan, like Iago and Richard III, has slowly been denigrated by his self-revelations. When we finally observe him "Coasting the wall of Heav'n on this side Night" as he prepares "To stoop with wearied wings, and willing feet/ On the bare outside of this World" (III, 71 and 73-74), the physical distance suddenly put between him and us destroys whatever close identification we have made with him, and we await a description which will put his mission into a larger perspective.

The description is given by God, whose point of view we immediately adopt; and it includes details which, although necessarily omitted from the synopsis, determine the event's quality. (I am thinking still not of style but of content, insofar as the two are separable.) Satan is transported by rage, he is "our adversarie," his purpose is "desperate revenge," he has broken loose "Through all restraint," he will soon try to destroy or pervert mankind (III, 80-92). The picture is not a pretty one. The prediction that "Man will heark'n to his glozing lyes,/ And easily transgress the sole Command" (III, 93-94) ought, in the kind of reader Milton expected to have, to arouse pity (together, perhaps, with some contempt) and alienate sympathy further from Satan.

The alienation should be permanent. In the remainder of the poem, we are given few opportunities to identify with evil. In Book IV, when the focus is next on Satan, he "falls into many doubts with himself, and many passions, fear, envy, and despare; but at length confirms himself in evil." Later in the same book, he wonders at the "excellent form and happy state" of Adam and Eve, "but with resolution to work thir fall." In Books V and VI he is described from

39

Raphael's point of view; in Book IX he is described from Eve's. When we follow his triumphant return to Hell in Book X, his transformation into a groveling and thirsty serpent makes him ridiculous. The crucial point in the alienation of sympathy from him occurs, however, at the moment when we first see him from outside, through God's eyes.

Up to Blake's time, this manipulation of the narrative line evidently worked. Since then it often has not worked, and one is tempted to speculate why. Although a full explanation would be very complex, one element in it is certainly a change in the affective valences of certain key terms. The word "God," which formerly could be counted on to evoke a positive response, no longer regularly does so. The cultural agreement which, in spite of dissension about the details of Christian theology, permitted confidence that the giving of an assertion to God established its rightness beyond cavil has disappeared. In the same way, the naming of Satan in connection with an attitude or opinion no longer suffices to vitiate it. I. A. Richards has persuaded critics to distrust "stock responses"; and the decline of epic has resulted in a tendency to read *Paradise Lost* as though it were drama, so that what is said by the epic voice is largely disregarded and a disproportionate emphasis is put on what is done and said by persons directly involved in the action. In consequence, signals which call for particular responses are resisted, and each reader adjusts his interpretation to his own extraliterary attitudes. My immediate thesis, however, is that Milton's handling of the narrative events is so contrived as still to produce the desired response in perceptive readers who are not determined to cut Milton's cloth to a preferred pattern. If a lack of tact in Milton's style gets the backs of readers up, that failure cannot now be given attention. (I am thinking, for instance, of an alleged harshness in the tonality of Book III; but that too, in my opinion, is apparent chiefly to critics who have prepared convictions about the superiority of emotional love to clear-sighted charity.) On the whole, Milton's arrangement of the events is perhaps just what it ought to have been to produce the intended response, at least for his immediate audience.

Let us observe one final example of psychological tendency before proceeding to some general comments about the plot. We were drawn to the fallen angels in Books I and II because their desperate situation seemed to invite moral support. When Satan is no longer oppressed, defeated, suffering but is about to succeed in victimizing newly-created men (who because of their inexperience may be supposed easily vulnerable), the balance of need shifts. His power has grown to the point at which the preservation of cosmic harmony and the reader's aesthetic poise requires that it be checked. We ourselves may, of course, be abnormally unhappy, frustrated, rebellious; if so, we will be delighted to see aggression exceed due measure. If not, the desire for quiescence which Freudians call, rather ineptly in my opinion, the Death-Wish (or Sleep Wish) is likely to assert itself here. The emotional strain put upon us by the thunderously assertive quality of Books I and II has prepared us to welcome an assurance that the devil's machinations will be frustrated. Sensing that Satan's foray will inaugurate a whole series of further disturbances, we look instinctively to God, as he is presented in Book III, for relief. If we realize, with Irene Samuel,[3] that the scene is dramatic and not expository, and if we are properly receptive to the warm love of humankind embodied in the Son, the total result is likely to be satisfactory.

Yet clearly it is not always satisfactory to twentieth century readers. Evidently something has gone wrong, either in Milton's handling of the scene or, if not in the narrative plan, in the modern response to it. Where does the blame lie?

[3] Irene Samuel, "The Dialogue in Heaven: A Reconsideration of *Paradise Lost*, III, 1-417," *PMLA*, Vol. 72 (September 1957), 601-11.

The usual complaint is that the portrait of God is repellent. C. S. Lewis comments that "Many of those who say they dislike Milton's God only mean that they dislike God: infinite sovereignty *de jure*, combined with infinite power *de facto*, and love which, by its very nature, includes wrath also—it is not only in poetry that these things offend."[4] The remark is cogent and includes a large part of the total answer. The development of political democracy, like the post-Miltonic apotheosis of *eros* or mere kindness at the expense of charity, has been unfavorable to poetry which assumes that Divine authority is infallible. So, too, has been the emergence of an antirationalism which has made logical rigor suspect; God's speeches now appear coldly legalistic. Even Lewis prefers suggestion to demonstration in poetry. When, he remarks, we read about Sanctities of Heaven receiving beatitude past utterance from God's sight, or come to the phrase "Dark with excessive bright thy skirts appear," our objections are silenced.[5] But there is a third obstacle which is also terribly important.

That obstacle is the difficulty, in our time, of creating sympathy for unflawed goodness. In Milton's day, characterization was thought of chiefly in terms of decorum and consistency. In spite of the psychological realism of much drama, fictive credibility had not yet begun to depend heavily on a recognition that the imagined personage was very like the reader, or at least was equally "human." Rather the contrary: the traditional dramatic "types" were often abstractions of particular qualities, and the prose "characters" which had a brief vogue in Milton's youth were caricatures spun out of ideas about theoretical fitness. Between the 1660s and Milton's twentieth century audience stands the enormous body of prose

[4] C. S. Lewis, *A Preface to Paradise Lost*, London: Oxford University Press, 1960, p. 130.
[5] *Ibid.*, pp. 130-31.

fiction, which, because it is predominantly realistic, has stimulated an assumption that fictive persons must be "life-like." Concurrently, it has become increasingly difficult to admire goodness and much easier than formerly to like evil. We are revolted by Tennyson's Galahad, who confesses that his heart is pure, and we cannot understand Ruskin's rather archaic judgment that only in Henry V did Shakespeare create a real hero. On the other hand, Webster's Bosola has found partisans, and a movie gangster can be made appealing if he is given a limp or is caused to love a wife who suffers from a racking cough.

In the area of public morality, the change of expectation has by no means been wholly bad. Although in private life sympathy is not an adequate substitute for the cooler but more effectual charity, the modern readiness to empathize with flawed character has generated public efforts to assist such moral delinquents as psychologically disturbed youths and unwed mothers. For the appreciation of Milton, however, the alteration of ethical climate has been little less than disastrous. God is disliked because he is "too perfect," Satan is attractive because his faults make him credible, Abdiel seems stuffy, Adam and Eve become "real" only after they have fallen. The especially competent reader (I believe) is saved from these misinterpretations by an ability to soak in, through his pores, attitudes different from his own everyday ones and by a moral flexibility which prevents him from assuming that his own views are unqualifiedly right. In any event, the failure to carry the modern reader with him in Book III is not wholly Milton's fault and has little to do with the narrative plan. At most, the poet has solved too triumphantly a difficulty inherent in beginning with two books in which the desire of former angels to revolt against Perfect Goodness had to be made comprehensible.

From this point on the narrative skill flags at only two

points. The depiction of the Garden and the First Parents in Book IV is admirable, the temptation is magnificent—we understand easily both Eve's yielding to Satan's arguments and her weakness in doing so—and Book X appeals even to anti-Miltonists. Of the long dialogue between Adam and Raphael in Books V-VIII, only the account of the War in Heaven raises serious questions, chiefly because the Homeric and Virgilian models are followed too faithfully.

One additional, and serious, difficulty must be mentioned—what has begun recently to be called the intractability of the myth itself. If animated and searching discussion of the poem continues long enough (as, for example, it may do in a graduate seminar), in the end Milton's defender must sometimes fall back on the claim that "He did it as well as anybody could have." The reason is that all myths tend, when lingered over, to raise unanswerable questions.

The story of Orpheus and Eurydice will illustrate as well as any other. Why, we may inquire, was it stipulated that Orpheus should not look round at Eurydice until she had issued into the sunlight? Explanations are easily enough invented: that Orpheus had to earn reunion with his wife by showing firm self-control, or that the King insisted his promise be credited absolutely, or something else. Any answer, if challenged, may be developed further. Self-control (or faith), we may say, is a condition of successful marriage. But this is already farfetched and will become more dubious the further we push the matter. Orpheus may not look back for the same reason, probably, that Cinderella must not remain at the ball past midnight, that Pandora must not open the box, and that Psyche must not look at the face of the husband who visits her only after dark. All such interdictions apparently derive from an obscure human sense that incomprehensible limitations are put on human behavior; and the human institution which most vividly proclaims the feeling is taboo.

Because the Christian myth had undergone a millennium and a half of rationalization, at the most crucial point of all Milton successfully avoided difficulty. His careful explanation of the prohibition in the Garden, and of God's desire that the Parents be allowed the option of sinning, meets quite adequately the usual student objection that God should have prevented the sin by denying the Parents free will or by making every conceivable action lawful. Continued reflection leads to increasing conviction. The matter is different, however, with regard to certain other aspects of the myth.

One of these aspects has to do with the transition from virtue to sin. Mrs. Millicent Bell has argued that Eve could not have sinned unless she was already fallen: an opinion which so overstates a valid insight that the discovery of any origin for sin becomes impossible.[6] Nevertheless a belief in free will certainly makes the showing of motivation difficult, for the stronger the motive is made to appear the less we are convinced that the will is authentically free. The fall of Satan presents still more serious problems, a discussion of which must be postponed to Chapter VI. Once again, we get into trouble if we inquire what would have happened if either Eve or Adam, or both together, had resisted temptation. Suppose both had done so: would their merit have been inherited by all their descendants, as their demerit was, so that human history would have been altogether happy? Such a consequence would seem as unjust as, in the actual story, the penalizing of the sinful Parents' descendants appears to many readers. Or, perhaps, would every human being, in his turn, have made a choice between obedience and disobedience, with the result that some would have fallen and some have stood? In that event, by what arrangement would two distinct races have lived side by side on earth, especially since there must

[6] See Millicent Bell, "The Fallacy of the Fall in *Paradise Lost*," *PMLA*, Vol. 68 (September 1953), 863-83; and my controversy with her in the same journal, Vol. 70 (December 1955), 1,185-1,203.

have been frequent transitions of members from one group to the other? No limit can be set to the ingenious questions which might be asked. The point is simply that myths, by their nature, tend not to stand up perfectly under searching examination. Although the Christian myth is extraordinarily rich and extraordinarily well rationalized—after all, the best minds of Europe had worked at the task for hundreds of years —it contains "mysteries" which not even the superbly equipped intelligence of Milton was able perfectly to rationalize.

For the rest, the narrative plan is beautifully worked out. Dr. Johnson's judgment, in his *Life of Milton*, that the poem "with respect to design, may claim the first place . . . among the productions of the human mind," although perhaps extreme, is at least soundly appreciative; and his further assertion that the episodes of the war and of Michael's visit "are closely associated with the great action" and were necessary, one as a warning, the other as a consolation, supports the view that the error was rather—if anywhere—in execution than in planning the skeletal structure. Beyond this, the large movements of feeling, besides involving basic human emotions of the kind described in the preceding chapter, develop in an easy and natural way. Indignation and rebellion give place to a recognition that, after all, the universal economy has a powerful sanction; the evil impulses continue to be unruly, achieve an apparent success, and then again are discomfited; punishment follows transgression, reconciliation succeeds estrangement, and the poem ends on a note of sober hope. Within the narrative frame, the feelings have been allowed to achieve a catharsis which leaves them healthily adjusted to the world in which our extraliterary life must be passed—and all this within an aesthetic world which, like the universe created by the Son, despite its mass hangs delicately balanced on its own center.

46

CHAPTER III

....

THREE

EXAMPLES OF AFFECTIVE

TONALITY

Hitherto we have considered *Paradise Lost* as a whole. In chapters to follow I shall study successive two-book sections of the poem from differing points of view. The aim will be to discover the importance in the total aesthetic structure, and by inference in the total meaning, of affects and percepts. I hope first, however, to make plausible the notion that the epic is suffused with affective overtones. (The role of percepts will not need to be argued because the importance of images is already widely recognized.) One way of accomplishing this end will be to look, in turn, at three relatively short passages; at the first two without methodological precommitments, at the third more narrowly, with an eye for data of one order only.

The first passage is that in which we are introduced to the central human figures of the poem. Perched in the form of a cormorant on the Tree of Life, Satan surveys the Garden and then turns his attention to the Parents.

Two of farr nobler shape erect and tall,
Godlike erect, with native Honour clad
In naked Majestie seemd Lords of all,
And worthie seemd, for in thir looks Divine
The image of thir glorious Maker shon,
Truth, Wisdom, Sanctitude severe and pure,

Severe, but in true filial freedom plac't;
Whence true autoritie in men; though both
Not equal, as thir sex not equal seemd;
For contemplation hee and valour formd,
For softness shee and sweet attractive grace,
Hee for God onely, shee for God in him:
His fair large Front and Eye sublime declar'd
Absolute rule; and Hyacinthin Locks
Round from his parted forelock manly hung
Clustring, but not beneath his shoulders broad:
Shee as a vail down to the slender waste
Her unadorned gold'n tresses wore
Dissheveld, but in wanton ringlets wav'd
As the Vine curles her tendrils, which impli'd
Subjection, but requir'd with gentle sway,
And by her yeilded, by him best received,
Yeilded with coy submission, modest pride,
And sweet reluctant amorous delay.
Nor those mysterious parts were then conceald,
Then was not guiltie shame, dishonest shame
Of Natures works, honor dishonorable,
Sin-bred, how have ye troubl'd all mankind
With shews instead, meer shews of seeming pure,
And banisht from Mans life his happiest life,
Simplicitie and spotless innocence.
So passd they naked on, nor shunnd the sight
Of God or Angel, for they thought no ill:
So hand in hand they passd, the lovliest pair
That ever since in loves imbraces met,
Adam the goodliest man of men since borne
His Sons, the fairest of her Daughters *Eve*.

(IV, 288-324)

The Adam described here is clearly intended to arouse awe-filled admiration. Eve, although awe-inspiring too in her own way, is meant to evoke chiefly the responses appropriate to loveliness and winning manners.

The first visual impression we are given is that both Parents are "erect and tall,/ Godlike erect" (288-89). The erectness has moral implications sufficiently familiar to Miltonists: unlike the beasts, man aspires heavenward and raises his eyes instinctively toward his Maker. Contemporary readers would have grasped the meaning at once. For the rest, the description at first rather states meanings than projects sensory objects. The pair

> In naked Majestie seemd Lords of all,
> And worthie seemd, for in thir looks Divine
> The image of thir glorious Maker shon.
> (290-92)

Although we seem to be contemplating human beings, we are in fact being instructed about how we should react to images which will be offered later.

The point, I think, is important, since in our century we have been taught that the artist should "present" instead of "telling." Yet if the legitimacy of Milton's purpose is granted, a little reflection will help us to recognize the propriety of his method. What shape of nose, what color of skin, what light in the eye or nobility in the forehead would be an objective correlative of wisdom or sanctitude? These are the qualities which the accepted myth required Milton to project here. True, a stage director (of Dryden's *The State of Innocence and Fall of Man*, let us say) might instruct actors to "look wise and pure," and might then, if not at once satisfied, give explicit instructions which would modify the visual image until he was pleased: "Raise your chin a little more"; "No, no! Toe out; don't look as if you were searching for a pocket; stretch higher." Unless he was dealing with rank amateurs, however,

49

he would tend rather to say, "More self-confidence!" "Look as if you owned what you saw"; "More purity!" In giving the directions, he would be describing not a dramaturgical artifact but the inferences he wished spectators to draw from what they saw.

It is exactly so that Milton proceeds.

> In thir looks Divine
> The image of thir glorious Maker shon,
> Truth, Wisdom, Sanctitude severe and pure,
> Severe, but in true filial freedom plac't;
> Whence true autoritie in men.
>
> (291-95)

We are informed about the conclusions—rather affective than cortical—to be drawn from the visual image but are not, for the moment, given the image itself. Yet we *seem* to be looking, to have an object before our eyes. "Hee for God onely, shee for God in him" (299): we picture Adam, perhaps, as glancing about him with an air of dignified proprietorship and Eve as fastening her eyes adoringly on him; but the picture has not actually been drawn.

Details are to come in a moment. As transitional to them occurs the clause, "His fair large Front and Eye sublime declar'd/ Absolute rule" (300-301). What is properly descriptive here is merely the declaration that Adam's forehead was large (or perhaps broad) and his eyes raised from the ground. The first detail points forward to the rather limited visual sharpness which is soon to come, the second backward to the framework of meaning, partly rational and partly affective, within which we must limit the activity of our imagination. The following clause is almost purely descriptive: "and Hyacinthin Locks/ Round from his parted forelock manly hung/ Clustring, but not beneath his shoulders broad" (301-303). Only the adjective "manly" is interpretative here; for the rest, appearance is expected to be the embodiment of significance.

From this point on, sensory details are given together with the meanings they imply.

> Shee as a vail down to the slender waste
> Her unadorned gold'n tresses wore
> Dissheveld, but in wanton ringlets wav'd
> As the Vine curles her tendrils.
>
> (304-307)

"Slender," although sufficiently denotative to be visually rather precise, carries connotations of gracefulness as distinct from strength; "unadorned" may suggest innocent simplicity. Otherwise the specifications are mainly sensory. At once, however, the meaning of the image is made explicit: "which impli'd/ Subjection" (307-308). Because Eve's hair is wavy, we are to understand that she is Adam's hierarchical inferior—an implication, we now realize, which had already been insinuated in the simile of the vine. The subjection, however, is not forced but voluntary:

> requir'd with gentle sway,
> And by her yeilded, by him best receivd,
> Yeilded with coy submission, modest pride,
> And sweet reluctant amorous delay.
>
> (308-11)

Once more in these lines, which Landor admired almost extravagantly, we have the description not of sensory qualities but of attitudinal. If we allow images to form in our minds as we read, they are our images, not Milton's. For most readers, the involuntary imagery here is likely to be sexual, no doubt because of the phrase "sweet reluctant amorous delay"; but a mental picture of Eve with love shining in an averted face while Adam makes sexual advances is wholly arbitrary in the sense that the reader manufactures it, out of his own creative energy, to embody a meaning which is stated without visual equivalent. The stimulus thus offered to the reader's imagination is an aesthetic good: contact with the poem is kept from being passive, so that the experience is not that merely of "entertainment."

The same technique is used in what follows. "Nor those mysterious parts were then conceald" (312): if there is imagery of a kind in the denial that sexual organs were hidden, the pictures must be supplied by the reader. All Milton has done is to jerk away a veil; what lies behind it he does not tell us. But the lack of concealment is not accompanied by shyness: "Then was not guiltie shame, dishonest shame/ Of Natures works, honor dishonorable" (313-14). After a four and a half line digression on shame our attention is recalled to the ostensible objects of description by the phrase "Simplicitie and spotless innocence" (318); and this again carries vague implications about bearing. The passage ends with an image of Adam and Eve walking together hand in hand, innocent and lovely. The details, partly motor ("passd . . . naked on," 319), partly static ("hand in hand," 321), are once more evaluated, however, by such phrases as "they thought no ill" (320) and "*Adam* the goodliest man of men since borne/ His Sons, the fairest of her Daughters *Eve*" (323-24).

Let us consider the aesthetic significance of what has been observed. Although the minutiae of the discussion may be controversial, the gist, I hope, will not.

If Milton had been asked what he had accomplished in these thirty-seven lines, he might very well have answered that he had given an introductory description of Adam and Eve; and, indeed, in a loose sense of the phrase, this is what he has accomplished. More strictly, he has hardly described *objects* at all. We know that Adam and Eve are erect, that

Adam has a large forehead and hyacinthine locks which hang down to his shoulders, that Eve's hair, which is unbound, hangs in wanton ringlets down to her waist, that their sexual organs are exposed, and that their hands are clasped. Nothing more. If we have no ocular acquaintance with the hyacinth, we may fail to realize that Adam's hair is more tightly curled than Eve's. For the rest, we have formed attitudes which will help determine our reactions to incidents that are to follow. Whether Milton was consciously intent on telling us how to evaluate the scanty visual information it is useless and irrelevant to inquire. My own guess would be that much of the evaluation has crept in involuntarily, without the poet's becoming distinctly aware of it. The mental image Milton had of Adam and Eve, formed, no doubt, partly on hints given him by paintings and such writings as those Watson Kirkconnell has collected in *The Celestial Cycle*, but also partly on spontaneously developed ideas about archetypal humanity, existed in his mind along with feelings evoked by the image. Image and feelings were not separated, as I have separated them, into sensory details and inferred meanings. No necessity existed that they should be separated, for the view that poetry was "presentation" had not yet been formulated. The materials of poetry consisted of data *and* commentary, which entered the consciousness simultaneously, or nearly so, and were not analyzed into qualitatively different classes.

More important, the poetic work done in the passage is in large part done not by the reason but by the nonrational faculty which we inadequately call "intuition." When we observe an action we often recognize significance in it without having to perform an act of rational analysis. I see a man in conversation with another man make an impatient gesture, and I know at once that he is rejecting an opinion or suggestion which the other has offered. If the gesture is brusque enough, and the expression of countenance which accompanies

53

it sufficiently haughty, I may infer that the man is unpleasantly conceited. I do not, in stages, observe, reflect, and conclude; the significance is immediately in the datum. I have remarked elsewhere on the immense role played by the interpretation of sensory phenomena in the forming of human attitudes and have suggested that many of our judgments (of human character, for example) result from peripheral sense impressions which have been registered by the subconscious mind. In the passage we have been examining, the job of inferring is done for the reader, but it is done as he might himself have done it, without a delaying circuit through logical processes. Sensory impression and inferred meaning appear nearly together; the action of noting is not felt as distinctly prior to that of interpreting. The reader sees and understands at nearly the same instant.

An explanation of the poetic method can be found in the nature of the creative act. If literary creation were mimetic in the sense that the writer imitated merely the sensory aspects of objects, such an interpenetration of datum and significance as we have found would not appear. Again, if aesthetic contemplation progressed typically from sensory objects to inferences about meanings, we would expect a movement from stimulus to response to characterize most descriptive passages. Usually, however, as in the passage we have looked at, stimulus and response are registered pretty much together. Sometimes one precedes, sometimes the other, but we have no awareness of a sequential relationship. What happens typically in art is that meaning and appearance are generated more or less simultaneously. Of possible objects *this* suggests itself to the creative intelligence as most nearly right because the appearance embodies the proper inference and the inference is appropriate to the imagined object.

So, at any rate, the description of Adam and Eve must have arisen. Since Milton had never seen the first parents, he imagined them in such a way as to project the meanings implicit in the traditional story. We are offered a physically admirable man who (we infer) holds himself proudly erect, whose eye moves unapologetically over the whole possible range of vision, whose features are composed, whose bearing is self-assured, who seems totally unaware that he is naked, and we recognize at once self-confidence, dignity, an easy conscience, and much more. No activity of the discursive reason is necessary. We do not work gradually from sensory datum to logical inference: "Men who have sins on their consciences do not hold themselves proudly erect; therefore this man does not have sins on his conscience." We *feel* the qualities for which abstract nouns and adjectives are rough and imprecise equivalents. The inferences are so deeply and instinctively human that they are mostly the same for us as for Milton. If we object to Milton's descriptive technique, the reason is probably that we have accepted a post-Miltonic aesthetic, Poundian or New Critical or other. But Milton's aesthetic methods are by no means historically aberrant, and they accord admirably with our natural modes of perception.

Such, then, are the impressions made upon us by the first parents. These are also affected by the natural setting, all the properties of which are chosen to accord with the implications of the human portraits. The innocence of the first parents is imputed to the Garden mainly by stripping away whatever in postlapsarian nature tends to produce anxiety. Precisely those animals with which we associate danger— the lions, bears, tigers, lynxes, leopards—are introduced gamboling. The elephant, which we do not especially fear, is shown intent upon amusing his human masters. The voluntarism thus suggested spreads, by contagion, over the whole scene; we may imagine, retrospectively, something of the same purposiveness in the gamboling of the predatory beasts and the sly insinuations of the serpent. Other animals, of unspecified varieties, demonstrate their innocuousness by couching in satisfied repletion or chewing their cuds as they seek resting places for the night. The lion dandles in his paw the kid which in the world of normal human experience is his prey. The physical strength of aboriginal man is paralleled by the strength of the animals, and his innocence is reflected in their harmless gaiety.

To what extent does the little scene have a rational structure? The reason, certainly, grasps easily what the imagination has presented; but the choice of images has not, probably, been determined by a process of either deductive or inductive inference. What inference is involved had mostly been completed long before the subject came down to Milton. In the millennium, it had been said long ago, the lion will lie down with the lamb; and the young goat serves as well. The images were thus readily accessible in tradition and did not have to be thought up by a poet desirous of producing a picture of nature as yet untainted by evil. But indeed, the thought of an ideal garden involved, almost by logical necessity, the elimination of faults and contradictions in the gardens we know. In the gardens in which human beings now walk and work, flowers are eaten by snails, berries are destroyed by birds; the birds may be stalked by cats, the cats by dogs; the ground must often be coaxed to bear vegetation, weeds choke out blossoms, roses attract aphides, stones turn the point of the spade. Once conceive of a perfect garden, and all these annoyances disappear as if by magic. Let the garden be wild, in the sense that it preexisted human cultivation, and the cats and dogs and birds which we see in the small plots attached to urban homes grow by a kind of internal momentum to the lions, lynxes, leopards, elephants, and snakes which we know to exist in untamed jungles; but here they offer no threat. The images of such creatures not noxious implies

ideality directly. If we think of peace and harmony simultaneously with wild nature, pictures like those Milton has
offered spring to the mind unbidden. What is necessary for
the poetic activity in the scene is not extraordinary power of
thought but a lively power of envisaging.

The second illustrative passage invites a different kind of
analysis. Every reader of the last hundred-odd lines of Book
XII (552-649) must feel that the poem is ending, that its circle
is coming full and its energy is about to subside. I hope to
show that the realization is produced by means which, although again accessible to rational understanding, are themselves rather affective than rational.

One element in the poetic technique is the use of words
which suggest descent from a height. Adam has been led by
Michael to a mountain top in Book XI:

> So both ascend
> In the Visions of God: It was a Hill
> Of Paradise the highest, from whose top
> The Hemisphere of Earth in cleerest Ken
> Stretcht out to amplest reach of prospect lay.
> (376-80)

On this height Adam has been instructed in the whole
future history of his people from the Fall to the self-immola-
tion of Christ and the Second Coming. As he descends from
the mountain with the angel, the epic itself slopes to a
conclusion. We remember, perhaps, rather in our feelings
than in our minds, that the poet had hoped to "soar/ Above
th' *Aonian* Mount" while he pursued "Things unattempted
yet in Prose or Rime" (1, 14-16). Now the soaring has ended
and we are being returned to the plane of everyday experience.
The descent from the mountain accomplished, Adam runs to
the bower where Eve has lain sleeping and then, still guided

57

by Michael, descends further with her "To the subjected Plaine" (xii, 640) which lies beneath Earthly Paradise. Nine lines later the work ends.

The physical action invented for the end of Book XII thus motivates a frequent use of words and phrases which evoke in the reader an impression of coming back to earth, of settling down, of relaxing from strain. "Let us descend," says Michael, "now therefore from this top/ Of Speculation" (588-89). Accordingly, "they both descend the Hill;/ Descended, *Adam* to the Bowre where *Eve*/ Lay sleeping ran before" (606-608). In the meantime, a band of cherubim has remained aloof from the central actors on another hill (xi, 208-10); these now descend "from the other Hill/ To thir fixt Station" and glide across the level ground "meteorous, as Ev'ning Mist/ Ris'n from a River ore the marish glides" (626-30). Michael then "catches" the "lingring Parents" and "to th' Eastern Gate/ Led them direct, and down the Cliff as fast/ To the subjected Plaine; then disappeerd" (637-40). His energy suggests an eagerness to have done, to get back to his usual station in Heaven, to bring matters to a new stasis; and his disappearance removes from view the epic personage who has dominated the falling action. Other phrases, like "Som natural tears they dropd" (645), add imperceptibly to the downward impetus (it would have been as natural to write "shed" or "wept"). The cumulative effect of all this is to produce an almost muscular sense of lowered tension and release.

A second strategy involves the closing off of narrative time. This sequence is introduced by a speech of Adam's:

> How soon hath thy prediction, Seer blest,
> Measur'd this transient World, the Race of time,
> Till time stand fixt: beyond is all abyss,
> Eternitie, whose end no eye can reach.
>
> (553-56)

If the only stretch of time which remains unexamined lies beyond human vision, the temporal limits of the poem have been reached. "I shall hence depart," Adam continues, "Greatly in peace of thought, and have my fill/ Of knowledge" (557-59). The motion of physical departure has temporal implications also; the ending of an action marks the completion of a time-span. "Henceforth I learne, that to obey is best" (561) points to a future which lies outside the epic frame. Many other phrases drive the impression home: "Th' Angel last repli'd" (574); "the hour precise/ Exacts our parting hence" (589-90); "We may no longer stay" (594); "thou at season fit/ Let her with thee partake what thou hast heard" (597-98); "The great deliverance by her Seed to come" (600); "That ye may live, which will be many dayes" (602); "evils past" (604); "He ended" (606); "But now lead on;/ In mee is no delay" (614-15); "This furder consolation yet secure/ I carry hence . . . By mee the Promisd Seed shall all restore" (620-23); "Ev'ning Mist" (629); "Homeward returning" (632); "looking back" (641); "Paradise, so late thir happie seat" (642); "The World was all before them" (646). Some of these expressions imply that narrative time is ending, others summarize a future which we are not to see; but all have a valedictory ring.

In addition to all this, the passage contains numerous metaphors of completion. "How soon hath thy prediction, Seer blest,/ Measur'd this transient world!" (553-54) The act of measuring is finished, ended. Adam has his "fill/ Of knowledge, what this vessel can containe" (558-59): the pouring is over, the pitcher will hold no more. "This having learnt," replies Michael, "thou hast attained the summe/ Of wisdom; hope no higher" (575-76). Adam has reached what for him is the highest attainable peak of knowledge. ("Summe" presumably has its Latin meaning, not the mathematical one which modern readers may assume.) When Eve is wakened, she says to Adam, "Whence thou returnst, and whither wentst, I know" (610). A journey has been accomplished; it was physical, but it was also a metaphor of search into the future significance of acts performed in the narrative past. The figure of the laborer returning homeward in gathering mists (629-32) is similar, although what the laborer has completed is an ordinary day's work, not an epic journey to a specular mountain. Most striking of all is the "flaming Brand" (643) placed over the gate of Paradise, within which all the terrestrial action of the poem has been set. If this is not, strictly, metaphorical, it nonetheless symbolizes the end of an important series of events. Henceforth the conditions of the parents' experience will be vastly different.

Taken together, all these details mean, inescapably, conclusion. The ways by which the meaning is implied can be explained rationally, as I have tried to explain them here; but only a dull reader can avoid feeling the approach to an end as he reads. Whatever small problems may be raised by the passage, its drift is admirably clear. The images and symbols all point in a common direction and do not, as in some recent poetry, demand critical interpretation before they can be grasped. The reason, I suggest once more, is that Milton was not victimized by aesthetic assumptions which caused him to inhibit the activity of certain parts of his mind. He drew no invidious distinction between sensory and cortical materials and therefore allowed his feelings to work in full cooperation with his intelligence. But this is to say that feelings, as well as thoughts, are embodied in his poem and can be made the object of study.

The third and final illustration will be based on a very brief passage—the poem's opening five and a half lines, which do not even constitute a whole sentence—and will be focused quite narrowly on syntactical data and their implications for oral reading, and on these alone. The passage, moreover,

was chosen before it was distinctly known to contain ana-
lyzable affections. The intention this time is to suggest that
a systematic approach of the kind to be made in succeeding
chapters may perhaps yield interesting results. The passage
runs as follows:

> Of Mans First Disobedience, and the Fruit
> Of that Forbidd'n Tree, whose mortal tast
> Brought Death into the World, and all our woe,
> With loss of *Eden*, till one greater Man
> Restore us, and regain the blissful Seat,
> Sing Heav'nly Muse . . .

It is a beginning that we all know (perhaps by heart) and,
it may be, have long since ceased to examine freshly at each
reading. If we approach it from a predetermined direction,
can we arrive at new insights? Our focus will be syntax and
its implications for feeling.

The opening three words, "Of Mans First," are strongly
emphatic: a light first syllable like the quick backswing of
a hammer, and then two solid taps, since "Mans" takes the
ictus and "First" contains an important meaning. As a prepo-
sition which introduces something of greater value than itself,
"Of" is spoken at a relatively low pitch; the voice rises on
"Mans," then as we come upon the emphatic "First" we find
that the higher pitch must be maintained. Further, we look
forward to a grammatical resolution, to the subject-verb combination which will give us something solid to hook the phrase
to, and in the meantime we keep the vocal curve unresolved.

The next three words, "and the Fruit," prolong the suspension but may trick us into dropping the voice prematurely.
We feel, perhaps, that the balancing of the three words "Mans
First Disobedience" with another three-word phrase creates
a reciprocation that motivates a downward curve to balance
the upward one. Moreover, the end of the line, coming be-

fore we have gained enough experience of the epic to be confident that the poet will be able to keep the rhythm flowing across line-ends, makes us want to mark vocally the point at which our eyes must turn back to the lefthand margin. But, in fact, by itself "and the Fruit" is meaningless and requires completion by the next phrase, "Of that Forbidd'n Tree." On subsequent readings we may compromise the contradictory impulses by holding "Fruit" up in the air but marking the line-end by a brief pause.

After "Tree," again, we expect the syntax to be resolved. While a part of the mind has noted the three-word equivalence of "and the Fruit" to "Mans First Disobedience," another part may have recognized the lack of parison (auditory balance) and therefore may desire additional syllables to create an acoustic equivalence which will reflect the syntactical one. "Mans First Disobedience" has six syllables ("-ience" is a monosyllable), "and the Fruit" only three. But a way of fleshing out the latter phrase has been provided by the dependence of "Fruit" on the prepositional phrase which follows it. We may thus read in either of two ways:

> Of
>> Mans First Disobedience, (3 words)
>> and the Fruit   (3 words)
>>> (of that Forbidd'n Tree),

or

> Of Mans First Disobedience,   (7 syllables)
> and the Fruit of that Forbidd'n Tree, (9 syllables)

If we choose the first, we think of the phrase I have put into parentheses as something thrown into an otherwise roughly balanced structure which delays the grammatical resolution momentarily. If the second, the latter and slightly longer unit also prepares us for a resolution after "Tree." The resolution is already two syllables overdue.

Again we are frustrated, teased. (It will be understood, I trust, that in order to make such points at all I must overstate them, sometimes grossly.) "Tree" unexpectedly generates a relative clause which has a transitive verb, "Brought," that after seeming to be completed by a direct object, "Death into the World," adds, gratuitously it may seem, a second object, "and all our woe." Its energy not yet exhausted, the clause next throws out a third prepositional phrase, "With loss of *Eden*," which looks back across both the intervening objects to "Brought." And grammatical resolution is still further delayed. The whole syntactical unit depending on the initial "Of," which has pressed forward clear through "loss of *Eden*," continues to hang in the air. At this point, however, we are again shot off at a tangent with "till one greater Man/ Restore us, and regain the blissful Seat."

The poem, evidently, is anxious not to oversimplify. It dallies, adds specifications for the sake of being scrupulously full, maximally explicit. The resolution is once more postponed until a temporal limitation is added to the top-heavy dependencies already piled up. Within this fresh element there is again rough parison: "till one greater Man/ Restore us" (8 syllables) against "and regain the blissful Seat" (7 syllables).

The doubling of this additional vocal and syntactical unit, together with the earlier doublings (of the objects of "Of" and the direct objects of "Brought"), increases our satisfaction when the main verb is dropped in at last with the ringing of a protracted nasal which is kept briefly in the memory by the "n" and the "M" of the following two words: "Sing Heav'nly Muse." Still the syntax does not end but instead soars off, in a way evidently to be typical of the poem, into another clausal divagation the end of which we cannot foresee. Nonetheless we have been allowed once to touch base and can leave it with some confidence that the remainder of the sentence will not cause us to be stranded.

The effect of such syntactical complexity is to suggest not merely powerful energy but also another quality which can best be called aspiration. The energy is evident in the reluctance to complete syntactical elements, the pressure of mind which spawns second objects of prepositions, a second direct object, an additional prepositional phrase, and two dependent clauses, the second with a compound predicate. But this energy must have a source, and we infer that the poet has gathered his strength to attack a subject which seems to him extraordinarily important. We are therefore not surprised when, as we read on, we learn that he intends to sing an "adventrous Song" (13) which "with no middle flight" will attempt to "soar/ Above th' *Aonian* Mount" in pursuit of "Things unattempted yet in Prose or Rime" (14-16). The invocation of the Muse who inspired Moses to write *Genesis* and the later address to the Holy Spirit who made the vast abyss pregnant and is now invited to do the same thing for the poet's chaotic mind nails down the impression that some enormous task is beginning; but the groundwork is laid in the complex syntax of the opening five and a half lines.

We do not, of course, normally pause to study the syntax as I have done here. The affective significance of the passage is embodied in forms that work upon our awareness indirectly, so that we are not distinctly conscious of what we have sensed. One of the special characteristics of literature, as opposed to mere writing, is precisely that its meanings are richer and more variant than its statements. The ways in which the meanings are communicated resist easy analysis; but if criticism is to perform a useful function, it can sometimes address itself profitably to those aspects of literary works which, although hard to talk about—and therefore hard even to cognize—are chiefly responsible for the works' status as literature.

In the chapters to follow the analytic method will resemble at first that used on the third illustrative passage, later those used on the first and second; but instead of combing through the poem for whatever may seem worthy of attention we shall consistently be in search of something specific. There are two main reasons for the adoption of this plan. The first, which is itself wholly adequate, is that explication of the kind just attempted is terribly expensive of space. If the whole poem were to be treated like the 141 lines just discussed, some 1,079 pages would be required—and that in spite of the fact that the second, and longest, passage was neither cited in the text nor examined at all exhaustively. I am eager to avoid the temptation to pay attention only to high spots, for a great deal of Milton's art is devoted to preparing for them and leading away from them. Secondly, I wish to test the belief that our recognition of affective and perceptual content will profit from the adoption of approaches likely to bring wanted data into prominence.[1] My special hope is by systematic study to arrive at fresh knowledge and not merely to demonstrate persuasively insights which I had previously attained. It is an aim which I think not inappropriate for use on a poem which has already been exhaustively investigated. The object of search will be consistently meanings which are nonlogical, nondiscursive; and these are, I take it, mainly of two kinds, affective and perceptual.

[1] The approaches have been developed from aesthetic assumptions developed in my *Literature and the Irrational*. Readers acquainted with that study will perceive readily that I attempt here to find in Milton, an unusually rational poet, affective and perceptual qualities asserted in the earlier book to characterize all literature.

....

CHAPTER IV

ANIMISM:

THE EPIC WORLD AS

SENTIENT

Having in two chapters considered *Paradise Lost* as a whole and in a third analyzed briefly some of the ways in which nondiscursive parts of the author's psyche contributed to producing it, I want next to attempt some experiments in histology. In this and the following chapter the emphasis will shift from purport to certain basic constituents of Milton's epic style. Here we shall look in Books I and II, which are usually discussed with reference to Satan and the fallen angels, for evidence that in this superbly cultivated poem, the creation of a mind furnished with the best learning available in the seventeenth century and in many ways astonishingly modern, appear animizing turns of speech characteristic of "primitive" thought habits.

Since poetry originated very early in human history and tends to be strongly traditional, it can be expected to preserve traces of psychic habits common among our remote ancestors. One such habit, well authenticated by anthropology, is the reading of human consciousness into nature. Children too, we are told, instinctively impute life and sensitivity to inert objects.[1] We all know that savages imagine spirits to inhabit mountains, streams, and heavenly bodies, and we are aware that in historical times the Greeks and Romans, in their

[1] For evidence see my *Literature and the Irrational* (1960), pp. 75-79.

polytheism, retained clear vestiges of the ancient perceptions. If we are parents, we have also heard our children exclaim "Bad floor!" when a doll's head has been broken by a fall or have overheard them giving verbal directions to a toy. Does the imputing of consciousness to objects incapable of it appear in Milton's highly intellectualized poem?

We should note at the outset a recognition among the ancient rhetoricians whom Milton studied that linguistic structures are frequently irrational. Many of the rhetorical figures analyzed—for example, by Quintilian (*Institutio oratoria*, VIII, vi, 1-76; IX, ii, 6—iii, 107)—were known to be logically inaccurate, if aesthetically admirable, and for precisely that reason needed explication. Moreover, as a student of Latin, Greek, Hebrew, Aramaic, Syriac, Italian, French, and perhaps Dutch, Milton's awareness of linguistic forms must have been greatly sharpened. Careful attention even to a second language inevitably calls naïve assumptions about language into question. The concentration on linguistic forms required by the educational stress on Latin and Greek and the teaching of rhetoric continued into the nineteenth century and beyond. When "English" was finally admitted to the academic curriculum, emphasis was often put on the recognition of rhetorical figures in poetry because the older analytic traditions remained vigorous. Little risk is involved in guessing that Milton was far more conscious of the illogical ways in which language is often manipulated than the typical modern reader.

A second influence must also be acknowledged: the comparative respectability in the mid-seventeenth century of a belief in what would now be called vitalism. That God includes nature is in some sense implied by the third of His attributes listed in Book I, Chapter 2, of *The Christian Doctrine*, "IMMENSITY AND INFINITY," and by the seventh, "OMNIPRESENCE." If, as Denis Saurat thought, God "retracts" his goodness from parts of the universal whole to allow it self-determination (cf. *Paradise Lost*, VII, 170-71), it need not follow that natural phenomena never reflect their relation to Deity by responding exuberantly to good human actions or shuddering involuntarily at bad ones. In *Paradise Lost* nature is several times shown reacting to human events: when the wreath of roses Adam has woven for Eve fades on his learning of her sin (IX, 888-93); earlier, when at the actual transgression "Earth felt the wound, and Nature from her seat/ Sighing through all her Works gave signs of woe" (IX, 782-83); and again when more complicated natural phenomena result from Adam's eating of the apple (IX, 1,000-1,004). But systems of thought other than Christianity had provided a rational basis for believing that there was a degree of awareness in apparently inert substances. Hermes Trismegistus, to whom Milton referred in *Il Penseroso* (". . . oft out-watch the *Bear*,/ With thrice great *Hermes*," 87-88), had described the cosmos as the "visible God"; and his influence on the Renaissance, both through the Neo-Platonism of the second and following centuries and directly, after the translation of the greater part of the Hermetic *Corpus* into Latin by Ficino in 1471, was immense. Accordingly the animizing expressions to be pointed out may not only have been more consciously produced than most of the data which will occupy us in the present study but may have been somewhat less figurative for Milton than they are for us. Nevertheless the essential archaism of the techniques remains unaffected. Whatever traditional sanction they may have had, and however much tincture of "truth" may have been attributed to them in the seventeenth century context, they had their origin in remote antiquity and continue, in simpler forms, to be reinvented by modern children.

In choosing examples I shall try to avoid forced readings. Many animizing phrases are so unavoidable that we all use them in everyday speech. When Milton writes "Meanwhile the hour of Noon drew on" (ix, 739), we shall understand him to be saying merely "It got to be more and more nearly noon." Yet this substituted clause will itself suggest how irreducibly animistic much language is. The root "near" in "nearly" has a spatial meaning which few readers are likely to have noticed. I have asserted, implicitly, that some indefinable "it," by occupying in turn successive physical stations arranged as an approach, has moved steadily closer to identity with a quasi-personified Noon who stands in a specific geographical position. Every paraphrase of the first half-dozen attempted may turn out similarly. "Noon approached"; "Noon was coming on"; "Noon drew near": it may be some time before we discover a locution as nearly colorless as "It was getting to be noon." All language contains dead metaphors—although, admittedly, one cannot always be sure whether a specific metaphor is wholly devoid of life. The best procedure will be to move from doubtful cases toward unmistakable ones while omitting entirely expressions which only an over-excited sensibility might notice.

The animizing process occurs under minimal tension when, by means of a transferred epithet, something not gifted with consciousness is implied to have a feeling or mood. Some such transferences are so natural as not to attract attention. Phrases like "ambitious aim" (i, 41), "dreary Plain" (i, 180), "bold design" (ii, 386), and "proud Cities" (ii, 533) might perhaps occur in speech. Yet of course it is really the man, not the aim, who is ambitious, the human percipient of the plain who is made dreary, the maker of the design who is bold, the inhabitants of the cities who are proud. Without being aware of the process, we often attach to objects and actions the mental states of persons with whom they are associated.

When the process goes a little farther it becomes recognizably "poetic." "Suppliant knee" (i, 112) is an example.

So too are "unblest feet" (ɪ, 238), "oblivious Pool" (ɪ, 266), "gay Religions full of Pomp and Gold" (ɪ, 372), "Audacious neighbourhood" (ɪ, 400), "righteous Altar" (ɪ, 434), "th'offensive Mountain" (ɪ, 443), "the sleepy drench/ Of that forgetful Lake" (ɪɪ, 73-74), "repenting hand" (ɪɪ, 369), "Region dolorous" (ɪɪ, 619), "the Trading Flood" (ɪɪ, 640), and "the fatal Key,/ Sad instrument of all our woe" (ɪɪ, 871-72). For reasons we need not pause to analyze, many of these phrases—because of variations in readers' language-sense, I will not say all—are beyond the line which divides literary speech from colloquial. In my opinion the most dubious case is that of "Region dolorous"; but here the reversal of normal order is decisive. Although our impressions may remain unexamined, we sense that language is being consciously manipulated. A suppliant knee is the knee of a suppliant man, a knee bent in supplication, not a knee which itself has a favor to beg; and similarly with the other instances. By twisting language in this way to obtain poetic effect, Milton implied an intention to do something special with words; and his manipulation involved the lending of sentience to what in fact does not possess it.

Other animizing transferences lie somewhere between colloquial and literary quality, so that assignment to one or the other category is difficult. I list the following examples: "doleful shades" (ɪ, 65), "happy Realms" (ɪ, 85), "happy state" (ɪ, 141), "gloomy Deep" (ɪ, 152), "mournful gloom" (ɪ, 244), "happy Fields" (ɪ, 249), "unhappy Mansion" (ɪ, 268), "Fanatic *Egypt*" (ɪ, 480), "mighty Standard" (ɪ, 533), "foul retreat" (ɪ, 555), "solemn touches" (ɪ, 557), "proud imaginations" (ɪɪ, 10), "the easie yoke/ Of servil Pomp" (ɪɪ, 256-57), "happy seat" (ɪɪ, 347), "happy Ile" (ɪɪ, 410), "drearie Vale" (ɪɪ, 618), and "lonely steps" (ɪɪ, 828). Some of these may be doubtful; for example, "proud imaginations" (imaginations, wish-fulfillment fantasies, which are themselves proud, or which make the imaginer proud?); "gloomy Deep" (a deep which makes observers gloomy but is itself gloomy in the sense of being dark); "easie yoke" (a yoke which is easy to bear but is itself at ease because no struggle is being made to escape it). The process by which transference is effected can be inferred from two definitions of "dreary" in a standard desk dictionary: "1. *Now Rare*. Sad; doleful. 2. Exciting cheerless sensations, feelings, or associations; dismal, gloomy."[2] Although the two meanings are perhaps not historically successive, the first definition may be called semantically strict and the second "extended." Of course the extension is made easily; in common parlance we say "Merry Christmas!" "Happy landing!" In such phrases language appears to reflect a suppressed tendency to animize. Because of his rhetorical training, Milton would have been more likely (I think) than the typical modern reader to be aware that the expressions are figurative. Yet the result is a slight energizing of the verse by the filling of its smallest semantic units with vitality.

Another variety of animizing transference occurs in personification. The distinction is in the nonphysical or conceptual nature of the referent. "Wearied vertue" (1, 320), "fainted courage" (1, 530—"fainting" in most texts), "proud honour" (1, 533), and "considerat Pride/ Waiting revenge" (1, 603-604) are illustrations. "Oblivious Pool" and "happy Ile" are less abstract. Virtue and honor might be made the subjects of allegorical paintings; Virtue could be portrayed as drooping, Honor might be given an elevated chin and flashing eyes. The island or pool would have to be painted as itself, obliviousness and happiness being symbolized otherwise than by facial expression and posture. This again is a common stylistic device in the two books we are examining. I find the following possible instances: "Where Joy for ever dwells" (1, 250);

[2] *Webster's New Collegiate Dictionary*, Springfield, Mass.: G. & C. Merriam Co., 1958, "dreary."

"Immortal vigor" (ii, 13); "Fate inevitable/ Subdues us, and Omnipotent Decree" (ii, 197-98); "words cloath'd in reasons garb" (ii, 226); "everlasting Fate shall yeild/ To fickle Chance" (ii, 232-33); "deep on his Front engraven/ Deliberation sat and publick care;/ And Princely counsel in his face yet shon" (ii, 302-304); "the Reign of *Chaos* and old Night" (i, 543); "complain that Fate/ Free Vertue should enthrall to Force or Chance" (ii, 550-51); "so Fate pronounc'd" (ii, 809); "eldest *Night*/ and *Chaos*, Ancestors of Nature" (ii, 894-95); "when *Bellona* storms" (ii, 922), and "*ancient Night*" (ii, 986). There are also longer passages, of which at least one deserves quotation:

> behold the Throne
> Of *Chaos*, and his dark Pavilion spred
> Wide on the wasteful Deep; with him Enthron'd
> Sat Sable-vested *Night*, eldest of things,
> The Consort of his Reign; and by them stood
> *Orcus* and *Ades*, and the dreaded name
> Of *Demogorgon; Rumor* next and *Chance*,
> And *Tumult* and *Confusion* all imbroild,
> And *Discord* with a thousand various mouths.
>
> (ii, 959-67)

An early personification of Sin and Death is so elaborately developed as to become allegory: Sin springs from the head of Satan at the moment he decides to resist the Divine will; the union of Sin and Satan produces Death; mother and child, after opening the gates of Hell for Satan's escape, feel by mysterious sympathy his success in seducing Adam and Eve, build a bridge over Chaos, and come to Earth to plague mankind. But allegory, here as elsewhere, consists of the animizing of abstract concepts. Like other forms of personification, it activates poetry by injecting it with hypostatized energy.

72

Other uses of personification are disguised, sometimes almost beyond recognition. "Sad overthrow" (I, 135) is typical of one kind of problem. Is the action, or result of an action, to which feeling is assigned half-personalized? We know that the meaning is "We, the fallen angels, have been made sad by our overthrow," but that is not what the poet *said*; how do we sense what he wrote? Again, is there, or is there not, a hint of personification in "expectation held/ His look suspense" (II, 417-18)? In both phrases there is unmistakable linguistic heightening. The first might be spoken sententiously in conversation, the second would be appropriate, outside of poetry, only in old-fashioned oratory or rather pretentious writing. Whether either is animistic cannot be said confidently. "Warr hath determind us" (II, 330) probably lies on one side of these two phrases, "here Nature first begins/ Her fardest verge, and *Chaos* to retire" (II, 1,037-38) on the other, and more figurative, side.

A cluster of other excerpts may leave us similarly perplexed: "when the Scourge/ Inexorably, and the torturing houre/ Calls us to Penance" (II, 90-92); "*Satan*, whom now transcendent glory rais'd/ Above his fellows" (II, 427-28); "With reason hath deep silence and demurr/ Seis'd us" (II, 431-32); "what time his Pride/ Had cast him out from Heav'n, with all his Host" (I, 36-37); and "each his several way/ Persues, as inclination or sad choice/ Leads him" (II, 523-25). Much depends as we read such passages on the flexibility and sensitivity of our imaginations. It seems to me not impossible that the seizure of the devils by silence and "demurr" can appear to have a trace of muscular quality, and that the casting of Satan's host out of Heaven by pride implies a sort of vitalism in pride itself; but every reader must make up his own mind. The *raising* of Satan by glory, the *leading* of the Devils their separate ways by inclination or choice, and the *calling* of them to penance by the scourge and the torturing hour in-

73

vite each its separate response, about which it would be folly to dogmatize.

The discussion has moved into an area in which, while the critic feels his way hesitatingly, his reader may suspect there is no footing at all. If, however, I am right in thinking that poetic energy must be sought partly in subliminal perceptions, this is one area in which investigation can hopefully probe. The language of literature is not logically precise. Probably it is less precise than the ordinary speech of educated people. Milton's reasons for preferring "what time his Pride/ Had cast him out from Heav'n" to the more rationally correct but less vigorous phrase, "when he was cast out from Heaven because of his pride", cannot have been that he thought pride to have been a physical agent of Satan's ejection. The hypostatization of abstract qualities characteristic of philosophical realism (which we now, because of a shift in point of view, call idealism) did not go so far as to lend physical muscles to psychological attitudes. Similarly the remark in *Lycidas* about plucking unripe berries and shattering leaves with forced fingers is not a rationally accurate way for the poet to acknowledge a feeling of unreadiness. The association of poetry with chosen plants depends on convention, not on necessary involvement. The point is that whereas we understand, roughly, why the passage from *Lycidas* is better than its logical equivalent we cannot say confidently what Milton gains by personifying Pride. Modern criticism is at ease in talking about sensory richness, image clusters, and symbols but does not possess analytical tools capable of estimating the vigor of personifications. I can therefore only propose, tentatively, that the quasi-personification of a mental attitude, even when so incomplete that the description as personification may appear strained, nudges the reader toward a kind of animistic perception to which, however much his education may have affected his everyday psychic habits, he is biologically predisposed. One or two such figures would no doubt have little power; but when a poem abounds in them the fit reader may gradually cease to resist an effect which by accumulation ceases to be negligible.

Further transferences, all of which in varying degrees assist the humanizing of perception, can best be noticed in the order of occurrence. In "the Fruit/ . . . whose mortal tast/ Brought Death into the World, and all our woe" (I, 1-3), causing is sensed as bringing or leading. A little farther down the page, where "cause" itself appears, it is said, transitively, to "move" the persons on whom it operates: "what cause/ Mov'd our Grand Parents" (I, 28-29). Thunder is personified as a wrathful archer:

> the Thunder,
> Wingd with red Lightning and impetuous rage,
> Perhaps hath spent his shafts, and ceases now
> To bellow through the vast and boundless Deep.
>
> (I, 174-77)

Orion is also armed, but with winds instead of arrows: "with fierce Winds *Orion* armd/ Hath vext the Red-Sea Coast" (I, 305-306). Aside from the phrases quoted earlier, I can find in Book I only two additional instances of personification or transference, both muted. "When Night/ Dark'ns the Streets" (I, 500-501) is possibly too colorless to be cited, and "Thir Glory witherd" (I, 612), if it implies internal vitality in glory itself, as in flowers or bushes—a vitality subject to desiccation and death—does so without insistence.

In Book II, which describes the rousing of the devils from passivity to further resistance, instances are more numerous. "The happier state/ In Heav'n, which follows dignity" (II, 24-25) is basically a transferred epithet but is brightened slightly by the metaphorical activity in "follows" and the quasi-personification of "dignity." Anger is personalized in a speech by Moloch:

> what doubt we to incense
> His utmost ire? which to the highth enrag'd,
> Will either quite consume us, and reduce
> To nothing this essential.
>
> (II, 94-97)

Belial picks up the figure in a retort which proceeds also to impute spontaneous will to God's breath and to vengeance. Will God, he inquires, through impotence or unawareness, let loose all his ire at once

> To give his Enemies thir wish, and end
> Them in his anger, whom his anger saves
> To punish endless?
>
> (II, 157-59)

What (he asks) if the breath that kindled Hellish fires

> Awak't should blow them into sev'nfold rage
> And plunge us in the Flames? or from above
> Should intermitted vengeance Arme again
> His red right hand to plague us?
>
> (II, 171-74)

The condemnation by the epic voice of the "ignoble ease, and peaceful sloath" proposed, in "words cloath'd in reasons garb" (II, 226-27), by Belial, is by no means inertly phrased. Other excerpts from this speech will claim our attention later.

In what follows we shift back for a time to weaker locutions. We hear only of "the Majesty of darkness" (II, 266) and are threatened with "Untam'd reluctance, and revenge though slow" (II, 337). Satan then praises

> Great things resolv'd; which from the lowest deep

Will once more lift us up, in spite of Fate,
Neerer our ancient Seat.

(II, 392-94)

The image of raising—by "things resolv'd"—contains some
of the renewed spiritual energy which has been produced by
the adoption of an offensive strategy. The council having been
adjourned, some of the Devils compete in martial games.

As when to warn proud Cities warr appears
Wag'd in the troubl'd Skie, and Armies rush
To Battel in the Clouds, before each Van
Prick forth the Aerie Knights, and couch thir spears
Till thickest Legions close; with feats of Arms
From either end of Heav'n the welkin burns.

(II, 533-38)

Clouds sometimes battle in the sky as the Devils do in Hell,
so that the welkin flames with warlike exploits; fingers of
darkness reaching out from the approaching masses are ani-
mized into knights holding spears. The songs meanwhile
sung by other devils, although querulous in import, have their
own hyperbolically figurative force:

the harmony
(What could it less when Spirits immortal sing?)
Suspended Hell, and took with ravishment
The thronging audience.

(II, 552-55)

Philosophy, too, even though false, can

excite
Fallacious hope, or arm th' obdured brest
With stubborn patience as with triple steel.

(II, 567-69)

77

The poet's energy flows so strongly into the most abstract concepts (harmony, philosophy) that they too are vitalized.

What is true of the devils' activities is true also of Hell itself, of Sin, of Chaos, and of Death. Far from being mere deprivation of good, Hell is a universe of death

> Where all life dies, death lives, and Nature breeds,
> Perverse, all monstrous, all prodigious things,
> Abominable, inutterable, and worse
> Then Fables yet have feignd, or fear conceiv'd.
>
> (II, 624-27)

Death is alive; Nature gives birth to monsters worse than Fables have pretended or Fear suggested. The coming into existence of sin is figured as a violent and self-generating birth: Satan's head

> flames thick and fast
> Threw forth, till on the left side op'ning wide,
> Likest to thee in shape and count'nance bright,
> Then shining heav'nly fair, a Goddess armd
> Out of thy head I sprung.
>
> (II, 754-58)

At this event "amazement seis'd/ All th' Host of Heav'n" (II, 758-59). Chaos, when Satan ventures forth into it, is lent feminine attributes; it is "The Womb of Nature and perhaps her Grave" (II, 911). The image, if vividly imagined, is unpleasantly strong: Nature emerges from a disembodied womb and later disappears into it forever. Across such a Chaos, Sin and Death, bestirring themselves in a way Dr. Johnson thought improper for abstractions, later paved after Satan's tracks "a broad and beat'n way/ Over the dark Abyss, whose boiling Gulf/ Tamely endur'd a Bridge of wondrous length" (II,

1,026-28).[3] Everywhere in the two books there is astonishing vitality.

So far the discussion has been chiefly preparatory. As yet only transferred epithets and instances of frank or disguised personification have been considered. The animism is less artfully indirect when objects *qua* objects are shown acting with self-generating energy.

The phrase "Words interwove with sighs found out thir way" (I, 621) is a case in point. When lingered over, the passage suggests that, although weakened by depression, the words struggle successfully against resistance. In Homer, we remember, words are sometimes "winged (ἔπεα πτερόεντα), and again they "escape the barrier" of teeth (ἔπος φύγεν ἔρκος ὀδόντων). The windbox of an organ is metaphorized into a human diaphragm: "As in an Organ from one blast of wind/ To many a row of Pipes the sound-board breathes" (I, 708-709). Other manufactured objects are treated in analogous ways. An altar "breathes/ Ambrosial Odours and Ambrosial Flowers" (II, 244-45), Soft pipes "charm" painful steps (I, 561-62). Banners, spears, and shields rise without human agency:

> through the gloom were seen
> Ten thousand Banners rise into the Air
> With Orient Colours waving: with them rose
> A Forrest huge of Spears: and thronging Helms
> Appeard, and serried Shields in thick array.
>
> (I, 544-48)

When swords are drawn, they "fly" out of their scabbards: "out-flew/ Millions of flaming swords" (I, 663-64). The blare

---

[3] Compare *Pontem indignatus Araxes*, *Aeneid* viii, 728. Quintilian calls attention to this phrase in the passage quoted in the last paragraph of the present chapter.

of trumpets produces itself spontaneously: "Sonorous mettal blowing Martial sounds" (I, 540); "the sounding Alchymie" (II, 517). Milton's poem itself has intentions and pursues high aspirations:

> my adventrous Song,
> That with no middle flight intends to soar
> Above th' *Aonian* Mount; while it persues
> Things unattempted yet in Prose or Rime.
> (I, 12-16)

The fall of an image of Dagon in the presence of the Ark of the Covenant (I Sa. v, 5) is ascribed to unfriendly energy in the Ark: "Next came one/ Who mournd in earnest, when the Captive Ark/ Maimd his brute Image" (I, 457-59). The palace of Pandaemonium, although built by devils, appears to rise by itself: "Anon out of the earth a Fabrick huge/ Rose like an Exhalation" (I, 710-11); "Th' ascending pile/ Stood fixt her stately highth" (I, 722-23).

Or consider the behavior of doors. Once Pandaemonium is completed,

> strait the dores
> Op'ning thir brazen foulds discover wide
> Within, her ample spaces.
> (I, 723-25)

The action is like that of the electrically energized doors of a modern supermarket. Although "The door opened" is idiomatic English, here the doors open "thir brazen foulds," not just themselves; the whole appears to inflict its will upon a part. The action of the gates of Hell, when Satan is preparing to issue from them, is similar:

> on a sudden op'n flie
> With impetuous recoile and jarring sound

Th' infernal dores, and on thir hinges grate
Harsh Thunder.

(II, 879-82)

So also is that of the Heavenly Gates. Says Chaos to Satan, describing the ejection of the devils from Heaven as he saw it:

Heav'n Gates
Pourd out by millions her victorious Bands
Persuing.

(II, 996-98)

The door of a Levite's house (*Judges* XIX) prefers one lamentable happening to another: "when the hospitable door/ Expos'd a Matron to avoid worse rape" (I, 504-505). The pattern appears in other books as well; in Book VI the crystal wall of Heaven, to facilitate the sweeping out of the rebel angels, "op'ning wide,/ Rowld inward, and a spacious Gap disclos'd/ Into the wastful Deep" (860-62). The vitalism of the gates spreads into walls. Beëlzebub ascribes self-confidence to stones: "Heav'n, whose high walls fear no assault or Siege,/ Or ambush from the Deep" (II, 343-44). Whatever objects are made by a conscious agent are likely, in this epic, to act of themselves.

It is the same with nature, with streams, the ocean, hills, and valleys. Rivers are regularly moved by a force more internal than gravity. The four rivers of Hell "disgorge/ Into the burning Lake thir baleful streams" (II, 575-76). Each possesses strong feeling: the Styx is a "flood of deadly hate" (II, 577), Acheron is "Sad . . . of sorrow, black and deep," Cocytus is "ruful," Phlegeton is "fierce" and its "waves of torrent fire inflame with rage" (II, 578-81). More to the present point, whereas smooth Adonis merely runs (I, 450-51), Lethe more characteristically "roules/ Her watrie Labyrinth" (II,

583-84). The sea divides "*Calabria* from the hoarce *Trinacrian* shore" (II, 661). The Red Sea takes action against the Egyptians: "the Red-Sea Coast, whose waves orethrew/ *Busiris* and his *Memphian* Chivalrie" (I, 306-307). Hills are sometimes violently active: "a Hill not farr whose griesly top/ Belchd fire and rowling smoak" (I, 670-71), and again

> thundring *Aetna*, whose combustible
> And feweld entrals thence conceiving Fire,
> Sublim'd with Mineral fury, aid the Winds,
> And leave a singed bottom all involv'd
> With stench and smoak.
>
> (I, 233-37)

The former hill has a humanizing "womb" (I, 673); in digging for gold in it, the devils open "a spacious wound" (I, 689). A valley wears vines for clothing: "The flowry Dale of *Sibma* clad with Vines" (I, 410). The vast pit of Hell has a "heart" (I, 151), will be unable to "hold" celestial spirits in bondage (I, 657-58), hears (II, 518-19), trembles (II, 676 and 788), and sighs (II, 788).

So everywhere with created objects, which are hardly ever inert. The firmament of Hell may "spout her Cataracts of Fire,/ Impendent horrors, threatning hideous fall" (II, 176-77). Chaos was "frighted" at the fall of the rebel angels (II, 994) and is the site of an eternal struggle of sea, shore, air, and fire (II, 912-14); it receives Satan "Wide gaping, and with utter loss of being/ Threat'ns him" (II, 440-41). Personified as a king, it keeps residence upon its own borders (II, 998-99). At the creation, instead of passively suffering formation out of the elements of Chaos, Heaven and Earth "rose" (I, 9-10). The heavenly bodies are sentient: the moon acts as a judge ("over head the Moon/ Sits Arbitress" [I, 784-85]), the sun "new ris'n/ Looks through the Horizontal misty Air/ Shorn of his Beams" (I, 594-96). Again, the moon feels the power of Lapland witches ("Eclipses at thir charms" [II, 666]).

Winds and other natural forces are similarly vigorous. In Chaos Satan meets "The strong rebuff of som tumultuous cloud/ Instinct with Fire and Nitre" (II, 936-37). Belial fears lest further insurrection may cause the rebel angels to become "the sport and prey/ Of racking whirlwinds" (II, 181-82) in Hell. Satan and Death, when a fight between them seems imminent, frown

> as when two black Clouds
> With Heav'ns Artillery fraught, come rattling on
> Over the *Caspian*, then stand front to front
> Hov'ring a space, till Winds the signal blow
> To join thir dark Encounter in mid air.
>
> (II, 714-18)

When the north wind "sleeps," dark clouds may "scowl," yet be dispersed by a friendly sun:

> As when from mountain tops the dusky clouds
> Ascending, while the North wind sleeps, orespread
> Heav'ns chearful face, the lowring Element
> Scowls ore the dark'nd lantskip Snow, or showre;
> If chance the radiant Sun with farewell sweet
> Extend his ev'ning beam, the fields revive.
>
> (II, 488-93)

Thunders may "roar/ Must'ring thir rage" (II, 267-68) and comets shake disaster upon the earth. Satan, we are told,

> like a Comet burnd,
> That fires the length of *Ophiucus* huge
> In th' Artick Sky, and from his horrid hair
> Shakes Pestilence and Warr.
>
> (II, 708-11)

Even a mineral may have indwelling vitality; we read of "living Saphire" (II, 1,050). (Savages, we remember, often believe that stones reproduce their species.)

The tendency, it will by now be apparent, is to perceive everything without exception as instinct with life. Parts of the body are endowed with a kind of personality. Satan's heart "Distends with pride, and hardning in his strength/ Glories" (I, 572-73); Belial's tongue "Dropd Manna, and could make the worse appear/ The better reason" (II, 113-14). Other abstractions than those already noticed are energized. The Holy Spirit, figured as a dove—a traditional result of the process on which the present chapter is focused—by brooding on the "Abyss," made it "pregnant" (I, 21-22). A climate is capable of giving metaphorical blows: "the torrid Clime/ Smote on him sore besides" (I, 297-98). The geographical north "Pourd never from her frozen loins" (I, 352) a multitude like that of the fallen angels. Space, apparently of itself, "may produce new Worlds"; that it would do so "There went a fame in Heav'n" (I, 650-51). Precious objects can be "barbarous" and may be "showered" by a direction of the compass: "where the gorgeous East with richest hand/ Showrs on her Kings *Barbaric* Pearl and Gold" (II, 3-4). The vitality of devils is transferred to the place they inhabit: "at our heels all Hell should rise/ With blackest Insurrection" (II, 135-36). In the same way, "Heav'n surcharg'd with potent multitude/ Might hap to move new broiles" (II, 836-37). Uncreated night has a "wide womb" (II, 150). The temper of an abstraction can change ("This horror will grow milde," II, 220); certain devils investigate whether "any Clime perhaps/ Might yeild them easier habitation" (II, 572-73); a hubbub "assaults" Satan's ears "with loudest vehemence" (II, 953-54).

One final cluster of relevant passages may be added, all having to do with the four elements and their qualities. Each of the elements can act of itself. "Of it self the water flies/

All taste of living wight" (II, 612-13). If the devils should invade Heaven, "th' Ethereal mould [earth]/ Incapable of stain would soon expell/ Her mischief" (II, 139-41). Fire may rage ("these raging fires," II, 213) or be "Outrageous to devour" (II, 435); it may "scathe" forest oaks or mountain pines (I, 613). Air is "buxom" (pliant or yielding—II, 842); it can work cures ("the soft delicious Air,/ To heal the scarr of these corrosive Fires/ Shall breathe her balme," II, 400-402); and it too has the power of feeling ("the dusky Air/ That felt unusual weight," I, 226-27). As a group, the elements sometimes fight ("fighting Elements," II, 1,015); in mutiny, they are capable of tearing the Earth from its axis (II, 925-27). At a more abstract level the four qualities of the elements engage in combat:

> For hot, cold, moist, and dry, four Champions fierce
> Strive here for Maistrie, and to Battel bring
> Thir embryon Atoms; they around the flag
> Of each his Faction, in thir several Clanns,
> Light-armd or heavy, sharp, smooth, swift or slow,
> Swarm populous.
>
> (II, 898-903)

Like everything else in the poem, concrete or abstract, insensate or conscious, the very materials out of which creation was accomplished are given quasi-personal status.

In their totality these examples indicate how thoroughly Milton's epic is permeated with vitalism. From the first 1,853 lines of the work, chosen not because they seemed especially promising but for the purely mechanical reason that they came first, some 165 phrases and passages—many of them rather long—have been cited; a number which may astonish even persons who, like myself, would have granted in advance the probability that Milton might frequently animize. We can hardly be mistaken if we conclude that the technique is critically significant, that it bears some responsibility for the poetic vigor of the books. Although all language includes animizing phrases (my own very workaday sentences are by no means free of them), a large proportion of those which have been noted differ unmistakably from the locutions of normal prose or of speech. True, many of the devices can be given rhetorical names: personification, transferred epithet, and so on. Nevertheless grouping them all as animistic assists, I think, a fuller understanding of how they all work.

Of course Milton's language is more archaic than his ideas. For him the wills behind separate natural phenomena have coalesced into the one will of Christian Deity. Yet he writes *as if* there were intrinsic power in virtually every object and even in every idea, so that concepts too become sentient and active. Possibly he consented to a tendency awakened in him by creative excitement to perceive the universe as children and savages perceive it; or, again, he may have recognized, partly because it was traditional from immemorial antiquity and partly because he himself was moved by it, the superiority in poetry of irrational language to rational. My own less specific guess would be that while imitating his models he took satisfaction in the effects he found himself able to produce. In any event, polished student though he was, veteran of a reluctant academic struggle lasting years with the scholastic philosophers, and himself, in the cooler element of prose, sometimes a notably tough-minded thinker, he caused the reader of his epic to move consistently in a world charged with *pneuma*.

Thus much of Books I and II on which our plan required us to concentrate; but we may look ahead briefly to Book VII, where the tendency to animize is probably strongest. I limit myself to one long quotation, italicizing the most vigorously animistic phrases:

over all *the face of Earth*
Main Ocean flowd, *not idle, but with warme*
Prolific humour soft'ning all her Globe,
Fermented the great Mother to conceave,
Satiate with genial moisture, when God said,
Be gatherd now ye Waters under Heav'n
Into one place, and let dry Land appeer.
Immediatly the Mountains huge appeer
Emergent, and thir broad bare backs upheave
Into the Clouds, thir tops ascend the Skie:
So high as heav'd the tumid Hills, so low
Down sunk a hollow bottom broad and deep,
Capacious bed of Waters: thither they
Hasted with glad precipitance, uprowld
As drops on dust conglobing from the drie;
Part rise in crystal Wall, or ridge direct,
For haste; such flight the great command impressd
On the swift flouds: as Armies at *the call*
Of Trumpet (for of Armies thou hast heard)
Troop to thir Standard, *so the watrie throng,*
Wave rowling after Wave, where way they found,
If steep, with torrent rapture, if through Plaine,
Soft-ebbing; nor withstood them Rock or Hill,
But they, or under ground, or circuit wide
With Serpent Errour wandring, found thir way,
And on the washie Oose deep Channels wore;
Easie, ere God had bid the ground be drie,
All but within those banks, *where Rivers now*
Stream, and perpetual draw thir humid traine.
(VII, 278-306)

The Earth "brings forth" grass, whose verdure clothes "Her
Universal Face with pleasant green"; herbs flower suddenly,
"Op'ning thir various colours," and make gay Earth's "bosom

smelling sweet"; the clustering vine flourishes forth, the gourd creeps out, the grain stands up, the bushes appear "with frizl'd hair implicit"; the trees rise as if in a stately dance and spread their branches (vii, 315-25). And so, with greater or less metaphorical density, throughout the whole story of the Creation.

The reaction of some readers to such a passage as that which has just been quoted may be negative. John Peter, in *A Critique of Paradise Lost*, is very severe in discussing Milton's description, in Book XI (844-54), of the ark's coming to rest after the flood. The "tendency in the direction of allegory—towards personification and the embodiment of abstractions"—provokes, he remarks, two objections; it "often results in clumsiness," and "it encourages a strain in the poetry which is turgid and tortuous, which lacks the vividness and energy it should have." He continues:

> Observe how at first the verse is clotted with semi-personi-fications: the sun staring into a mirror and then sucking up the waters, the ebb 'tripping . . . With soft foot,' the deep like a farmer engaged in some mysterious form of irrigation, and Heaven a householder shutting out the rain. Only when the verse shakes off this integument of half-formed and jumbled images does the scene come into focus, and only then does it come to life: the rising crests of the hills, the run-off of water plunging and frothing down the valleys, and the line of the subsiding sea.[4]

From this point of view the animism we have been noticing is the opposite of an achievement. Milton sinks into it, presumably, when his creative energy is feeble.

It may be so. The minds of clever readers differ surprisingly, and not even a census of opinions can inform us reliably about

[4] Peter, *Critique of Paradise Lost*, New York: Columbia University Press, 1960, pp. 139-40.

what receptive attitudes are "most proper" or "best." My own
responses, however, so far as I can analyze them, are the opposite of Mr. Peter's; and I urge strongly that poetry should
be encouraged to do all it can to the mind so long as the work's
wholeness is not vitiated and the critic tries conscientiously
to exclude from his mind whatever is not in the poetic data
themselves. On first reading Book VII, where animism is
densest, may drag somewhat. One wants to get on with the
story, to find out what is to happen next. On subsequent readings, for me at least, the description is sheer delight. I do not
think the book has been praised sufficiently. For the reader who
does not shrink from sensuousness in poetry but is willing to
expose himself to a bombardment of half-living colors, shapes,
and feelings—who is not, that is to say, disoriented in dealing
with epic because he wants it to be drama or realistically
sensible, or both—Book VII can be an exhilarating, if
perhaps finally exhausting experience. Alfred Biese, in a little
nineteenth century book which I have cited elsewhere, long
ago suggested what I think is a chief cause when he said of
poetry generally, "The poet unlocks the shaft of hidden depths;
and his magical key is analogy, the anthropocentric, the metaphorical."[5] Milton might have found a hint with the same
import in Quintilian's *Institutio Oratoria*: "Above all, a
wonderful sublimity is produced by phrases which are elevated
by a bold and almost risky transference, when we impute a
certain activity and spirit to objects lacking sensibility, as in
'Araxes, resenting a bridge' " (VIII, vi, 11).[6] No hint, however,
is likely to have been necessary, for Milton was a true poet

[5] Biese, *Die Philosophie des Metaphorischen*, Hamburg and Leipzig: Verlag
von Leopold Voss, 1893, p. 94.

[6] *Praecipue ex his oritur mira sublimitas, quae audaci et proxime periculum
translatione tolluntur, cum rebus sensu carentibus actum quendam et animos
damus, qualis est 'Pontem indignatus Araxes.'* Quintilian wrote, however, in
a tradition; Aristotle (*Rhetoric* III, xi) had long before called personifying
metaphors "approved."

and could have felt, if he did not stop to reason out, the approach to dramatic vividness attainable by lending consciousness or the power of action, or both, to all his poetic objects and concepts without exception.

....

CHAPTER V

SYNECDOCHE

AND METONYMY

So flexible is language, so responsive to feeling, that it reveals not only the ideas and images which occupy the speaker's mind but also the affective values with which these are tinged. Most of the referents of words are sufficiently complex to permit description by one or more of a rich variety of terms; and the choices made among the possibilities often suggest both a selected aspect of the referent and an attitude evoked by the aspect.

An individual human being, whom we may call by some such name as Roy Jones, will provide an illustration. For the whole man, the only appropriate designation is the proper name. Only this isolates the individual sharply from the group and indicates the total bundle of actualities and potentialities which constitute his idiosyncratic nature. *That* is Roy Jones: we follow the pointing finger and see a man whom we would be able to distinguish from all other men in a different situation from the present one, or we recognize a human being we have met before. But Jones need not always be called by his name and very often is not. For his underlings in the office he may be the Boss. For his wife he is perhaps My Husband, for his children Dad, for his physician The Patient, for a saleswoman the Customer or The Prospect, for the Congressional Ways and Means Committee A Taxpayer, for a lawyer The Plaintiff or The Defendant, for a loan agency An Account, and so on almost illimitably. The tone in which the designations are spoken may be proud or affectionate or pitying or contemptuous or neutral. Whether Jones is happily married may perhaps be inferred from the way his wife says "My Husband" and the loyalty of his employees from auditory qualities in their pronunciation of "the Boss." Jones may also be indicated, however, within any of the innumerable relationships into which group living has forced him, by a wide range of other terms or phrases which carry recognizable feeling tones even on the printed page. Without utterance, such terms not only define a selected aspect of the complex human personality named Jones but also connote an emotional bias in the user. If Jones's employees refer to him as The Chief but his wife calls him That Skinflint and his daughter Old Curfew, we can infer that he is more respected at the office than at home. The very richness of language, indeed, forces on speakers and writers a continual choice among lexical possibilities; the result is that most speech and writing is affectively toned. Only certain varieties of governmental and academic gobbledegook come near to achieving emotional neutrality, and even there the coolness is usually less than was intended.

In old fashioned rhetoric, the designation of a person or object by one of its parts or aspects is called *synecdoche*, the designation of it by one of its properties or accompaniments *metonymy*. For the present purpose it is unnecessary to enumerate the subdivisions of the two figures or even to differentiate sharply between them. One or the other comes into play when we call a presiding officer "the Chair" or "the Speaker," workmen "hands," the written word "the pen" and military action "the sword" ("The pen is mightier than the sword"), the people of France "France" ("France was indignant"), the works of Shakespeare "Shakespeare" ("a copy of Shakespeare"), a sweetheart "my love," a ship a "vessel," death "the grave." Unless specifically excepted, the expressions to be cited in the remainder of the chapter all include terms which fall under one of these two general heads, although sometimes in a subclassification which at first glance may seem not to be covered by the definition. I intend in what follows to examine whether affective attitudes embodied in Books III and IV of *Paradise Lost* can be illuminated by Milton's use of these two rhetorical figures.

We can begin by observing words and phrases used of the First Person of the Trinity, who appears more prominently in Book III than elsewhere. The aspect of power is emphasized by "Omnipotent" (III, 372; IV, 86, 725) and "th' Almighty" (III, 273, 344). An awareness of familial relationship is acknowledged by "Father" (III, 372, 415). The two aspects are brought together in "th' Almighty Father" (III, 56 and 386). Authority is emphasized by "Heav'n's King" (IV, line III), "Eternal King" (III, 374), "thy Law" (IV, 637), and perhaps "Heav'n permits" (IV, 1,009). Timelessness, stressed secondarily in "eternal King," is selected for exclusive emphasis in "th' Eternal" (IV, 996). Creativeness—a wider function than parenthood—is suggested by "great Creatour" (III, 167, 673; IV, 684), "Maker" (IV, 725), "Author of all being" (III, 374), and, more restrictively, "Fountain of Light" (III, 375). A divine awareness motivated by friendly interest is implied by "bent down his eye" (III, 58) and "Mine eare shall not be slow, mine eye not shut" (III, 193). A willingness to temper impersonality with compassion is asserted by reference to "the strife/ Of Mercy and Justice in thy face discernd" (III, 406-407). Finally, "Immutable, Immortal, Infinite" (III, 373) is a serial epithet which recognizes three impressive qualities of the Supreme Deity.

The affective tonality of these designations is clearly positive. What Milton might have done is suggested by Satan's phrase "my punisher" (IV, 103). Omnipotence might have been alluded to by "Th' o'erwhelmer," authority by "Tyrant," timelessness by "Th' unexpir'd," creativeness by "The Spawner." And so with the rest. Evidently Milton has sought expressions which would produce in his readers an awed admiration, and perhaps also acquiescence; or, alternatively, the epithets issued from a mind in which access to pejorative terms was blocked by an affective bias.

This inference is strongly supported by an examination of the tonally contrasting epithets used of Satan. "Which way I flie is Hell; my self am Hell," says Satan of himself (IV, 75). "Wherefore with thee," asks Gabriel, "Came not all Hell broke loose?" (IV, 917-18). After yielding to death, Christ predicts, He will "through the ample Air in Triumph high/ . . . lead Hell Captive maugre Hell" (III, 254-55). Once arrived on Mount Niphates, horror and doubt stir the Hell within Satan:

> for within him Hell
> He brings, and round about him, nor from Hell
> One step no more then from himself can fly
> By change of place.
>
> (IV, 20-23)

Elsewhere (except when Gabriel addresses him contemptuously as "courageous Chief," IV, 920) Satan is the "adversarie" (III, 81, 156), "the Fiend" (III, 430, 440, 498, 524, 588; IV, 166, 285, 393, 857, 1,005, 1,013), the "bane" of the odorous sweets in Paradise (IV, 166-67), "ingrate" (III, 97), "the false dissembler" (III, 681), "the grieslie King" (IV, 821), "mortal foe" (III, 179), "secret foe" (IV, 7), "our Destroyer, foe to God and Man" (IV, 749), "this first grand Thief" (IV, 192), "The Tempter ere th' Accuser of man-kind" (IV, 10), "Artificer of fraud" (IV, 121), "the Dragon" (IV, 3)—a transparent allusion to *Revelation* 12:9: "the great dragon . . . that old serpent, called the Devil, and Satan, which deceiveth the whole world"—and "the fraudulent Impostor foule" (III,

692). His "desperate revenge," we are told, will "redound/ Upon his own rebellious head" (III, 85-86). When, in the Garden, he first hears Adam speak, he turns "all eare" (IV, 410) in his eagerness to find an opening for mischief. "Th' aspiring Dominations" (III, 392) evokes a slight curl of the lip because, in context, it reminds us that such aspiration deserved and received punishment.

The foregoing terms are all unmistakably derogatory. The thought of Satan and his cohorts is as repugnant to Milton as the thought of the First Person of the Trinity is welcome, if somewhat awe-inspiring. So far as the limited perspectives of the present chapter allow us to determine, the pronounce- ment of Landor stands justified, that "There is neither truth nor wit . . . in saying that Satan is hero of the piece, unless, as is usually the case in human life, he is the greatest hero who gives the widest sway to the worst passions." Milton has consistently chosen for Satan and his followers synecdoches and metonymies which imply disapproval and contempt.

Designations chosen for the Second Person of the Trinity, the Son, are in a different affective universe. As His Father's "effectual might" (III, 170), the Son is "The great Work- Maister" (III, 696), "glorious Maker" (IV, 292), and "sovran Planter" (IV, 691). The father's use of the Son as an agent for the pronouncement of divine decrees, and also His acknowl- edgment of the Son as a creative embodiment of wisdom, is implied by "Son who art alone/ My Word, my wisdom" (III, 169-70). The likeness of the Son to the Father is emphasized in "Divine Similitude" (III, 384) and "on his right/ The radiant image of his Glory sat" (III, 62-63). "Head Supream" (III, 319) announces the Son's delegated kingship. The affective overtones of other synecdochical and metonymical epithets are even more favorable. The Son's redemptive mis- sion is hailed in "Saviour of Men" (III, 412), and the ques- tion "Dwels in all Heaven charitie so dear?" (III, 216) provokes the Son to declare his readiness to suffer incarnation and death on behalf of man. The reaction expected from readers is implied immediately upon the conclusion of the Son's speech:

> his meek aspect
> Silent yet spake, and breath'd immortal love
> To mortal men, above which onely shon
> Filial obedience.

(III, 266-69)

The Son is therefore, as "the onely peace/ Found out for mankind under wrauth," understandably His Father's "sole complacence" (III, 274-76). Moreover, the pleasure of the Father in the love of the Son for sinful mankind reflects back on the Father a portion of whatever warmth is generated by the commendatory phrases used of the Son.

Beneath the persons of the Trinity, but above mankind, stand the unfallen angels, who except in Satan's slighting addresses to Gabriel as "Insulting Angel" (IV, 926) and "Proud limitarie Cherube" (IV, 971) are also spoken of eulogistically. As a group collected about the Holy Mount they are "Sanctities of Heaven" (III, 60). Successively thereafter they are "Heav'nly Powers" (III, 213), "All Heav'n" (III, 272), "Thrones, Princedoms, Powers, Dominions" (III, 320), "brightest Seraphim" (III, 381), and "Powers" (III, 397). A number of them who accompany Gabriel in a search for Satan in Earthly Paradise are described as "radiant Files" (IV, 797). Uriel stands in the sun as one of God's "Eyes" (III, 650). "Creature" (IV, 582), used by Gabriel as an epithet for any angel who might have passed by the sun on a visit to Earth, is apparently intended to suggest an acknowledged dependency on the Godhead. Satan himself, during his conversation with Uriel, is so effectively disguised as a good angel that

in his face
Youth smil'd Celestial, and to every Limb
Sutable grace diffus'd.

(III, 637-39)

With the exception of passages in which dramatic propriety
requires a fiend to speak slightingly of them, the angels are
regularly characterized by terms which attribute to them
qualities likely to evoke favorable responses.

Unspoiled humanity, represented by Adam and Eve, are
at first described as being "with native Honour clad/ In
naked Majestie"; in appearance, they are "Lords of all" (IV,
289-90). These expressions lie near or beyond the verge of the
rhetorical figures with which we are presently concerned; but
when Eve calls Adam "My Guide/ And Head" (IV, 442-43)
or "My Author and Disposer" (IV, 635), we are back on safe
ground. Eve, in turn, is called by Adam "individual solace
dear" (IV, 486), "Part of my Soul" (IV, 487), "Daughter of
God and Man" (IV, 660), and "Sole partner and sole part of
all these joys" (IV, 411). For the epic voice, Eve is "our general
Mother" (IV, 492); Adam is "our first Father" (IV, 495),
"our general Ancestor" (IV, 659), and "our Sire" (IV, 712).
Men generally—that is to say, Adam and Eve together—are
to be "Authors to themselves in all/ Both what they judge
and what they choose" (III, 122-23). Man is God's "creature"
(III, 151); Adam, until the Atonement, will be "The Head of
all Mankind" (III, 286). For Satan the pair are "Creatures of
other mould, earth-born perhaps" (IV, 360)—something made,
hence derivative, no doubt dependent, and perhaps vulnerable
to injury. In recapitulating her earliest experience, Eve calls
her image in the pool "A Shape" (IV, 461); and it is, in fact,
as a shape that she at first unwisely prefers herself to Adam.

The total effect of these nouns of reference is ambivalent.
In the main, our response is obviously intended to be favor-

able; but some of the epithets imply a vague threat. In the event, Adam is not to be Eve's "Disposer," but rather the victim of her disposing. The judgments and choices to be made by the two are not, we are aware, to be consistently wise. Although the "Shape" Eve sees in the pool is recognized to be deliciously attractive, in context the epithet arouses a slight discomfort, for she should not even momentarily prefer her own figure to Adam's. The earthliness of the two creatures, if not discreditable, at least suggests exposure to the superior power of a fallen angel. Other speeches evoke even more clearly a consciousness that Paradisal bliss is precarious. When the Father inquires of the Heavenly host which of them will be "mortal to redeem/ Mans mortal crime and just th' unjust to save" (III, 214-15), a fall is seen to be imminent; and the impression is deepened by the announcement that finally the world will burn and a new Heaven and Earth will spring from the ashes as a home for "the just" (III, 334-35), who are implied to be only a portion of total mankind.

In the Heavenly dialogue at the beginning of Book III, which sets the stage for our first glimpse of the Parents, Adam and Eve are regularly called either "Man" or "hee" and "shee"—nonfigurative terms of an emotionally neutral quality which, embodied as they are in a prediction of events that are not to occur until much later, do not predispose us to admire. Our view of human glory, when it comes, is all the more affecting because we know that the splendor will be transient.

So far we have been considering personages, superhuman and human; but metonymies and synecdoches may also be used of objects or actions. Sometimes the tonality is affectively neutral, as when Satan "wings his way" (III, 87) through Chaos. To be sure, it is "Through all restraint broke loose" that he does so, and perhaps some of the contempt in the phrase carries over to "wings"; but the verb itself may be taken as either laudatory or pejorative, depending on whether by this time we think of Satan as criminal or hero. Such phrases as "the Deep" (III, 586), "Th' Arch-chimic Sun" (III, 609), "moist and dry" (III, 652), and even "Heav'n" (IV, 676—for the stars and planets) carry little emotional charge, although the last may be vaguely commendatory. For the most part, however, figures used of actions and objects also tend to impute some degree of praise or blame.

How little is needed to weight the balance in either direction is seen in "Thee I re-visit now with bolder wing" (III, 13), which by qualifying the nominal form of a word just said to be neutral gives it emotional color—in this passage favorable, since the expression implies relief from anxiety. Darkness, which usually connotes evil, is made attractive in the invocation to Book III:

> as the wakeful Bird
> Sings darkling, and in shadiest Covert hid
> Tunes her noctural Note.
> (III, 38-40)

The associating of darkness with music is responsible for the tonal alteration. More often brightness suggests admirable qualities, as in the description of the guardian angels dividing into parties to search for an intruder:

> As flame they part
> Half wheeling to the Shield, half to the Spear.
> (IV, 784-85)

"Flame," besides naming the element of which angelic bodies are made, implies martial eagerness, and "the Shield" and "the Spear," for "left" and "right," indicate not only the imminence of conflict but also the preparedness of the angels and the concentration of their minds on the task in hand. Again, the addition of an adjective often suggests the desired tone, as in

"Harmonious numbers" (III, 38), "Celestial temper" (IV, 812), "A happy rural seat" (IV, 247), "gold'n days, fruitful of gold'n deeds" (III, 337), "the great Luminarie/ . . . That from his Lordly eye . . ./ Dispenses Light from farr" (III, 576-79), "loftiest shade" (IV, 138), "stateliest view" (IV, 142), "thy sovran vital Lamp" (III, 22), "Celestial Light" (III, 51), "the pure Empyrean" (III, 57), "coole *Zephyr*" (IV, 329), "the happie Garden" (III, 66), "immortal fruits" (III, 67), and "loftie shades" (III, 734). Other qualifying expressions are more ambiguous; but presumably "a tuft of shade" (IV, 325) is intended to offer relief from oppressive heat, and "pendant shades" (IV, 239) to suggest a protective drooping of foliage. In contrast, "Heav'nly love" (III, 298) hardly requires adjectival pointing except to attribute the affection to God, and "mutual love, the Crown of all our bliss" (IV, 728), by doubling the quantity of love and asserting its reciprocal character, prepares for the statement about crowning our parents' happiness. Rarely, a favorable connotation is insured by the rejection of an unfavorable one, as when the poet says of wedded love, "Farr be it, that I should write thee sin or blame" (IV, 758). In general, however, the epic assumes the audience's ability and willingness to interpret signals with little help. When the blest voices of the angels utter joy (III, 347), we are expected to accept the appropriateness of their emotion to the occasion. The time was still distant when joy might be a subject of derision and coprophagous figures might imply approval. In the seventeenth century the emotions were still mainly socialized, and the affective associations of roses and sunsets and skeletons relatively stable.

Other figurative expressions used of objects and actions are tonally negative. A low-pressured anxiety is awakened by Earthly Paradise itself: "thy abundance wants/ Partakers, and uncropt falls to the ground" (IV, 730-31). Already the poet is laying the groundwork for the quarrel which is to arise over efficient gardening methods in Book IX. Often the metonymical or synecdochical term itself is unpleasant; by referring to something disagreeable, it produces revulsion, sometimes fairly mild, sometimes vigorous; and the effect may be sharpened by an adjective. The following phrases are examples: "New *Babels*" (III, 468), "Through utter and through middle darkness borne" (III, 16), "cloud in stead, and ever-during dark" (III, 45), "the desolate Abyss" (IV, 936), " *Chaos* and *Eternal Night*" (III, 18), "And in the lowest deep a lower deep" (IV, 76). Again the noun may be colorless and the affective energy lie in the adjective, as in "th' unaccomplisht works of Natures hand" (III, 455) and "His fall'n condition" (III, 181). But there are many technical variations. In "they arraignd shall sink/ Beneath thy Sentence" (III, 331-32), "Sentence" has a good connotation, but precisely because it does, the spirits who incur judgment are known to be bad. "My Vanquisher" (III, 251), who is Death, is traditionally evil but all the more repugnant here because his victim is Christ. Depression arises in the following passage from the privation of something good: light does not revisit the poet's eyes,

> that rowle in vain
> To find thy piercing ray, and find no dawn:
> So thick a drop serene hath quencht thir Orbs.
>
> (III, 23-25)

Fearfulness in good angels—not an evil, but a lack of active good—is implied by the unwillingness of each to draw "upon his own head . . ./ The deadly forfeiture" (III, 220-21). The range of technical possibility is wide.

Although the words "synecdoche" and "metonymy" have vague boundaries, so that a resurvey of Books III and IV by another student might yield additional examples, the evidence has now been virtually exhausted. No attempt has been made to suppress awkward figures; yet the findings all point unmistakably in a single direction. Like all of us in common speech, but more frequently, since he was a poet, Milton has referred to things by terms which indicated some one of their aspects or accompaniments; and his choices have indicated an affective bias of exactly the kind which traditional criticism has always recognized. When thinking of Satan, he has been reminded of evil or Hell; when thinking of God or the Son, he has had impressions of benevolent power and light; the faithful angels have evoked responses to sanctity, obedience, and brightness. To be sure, the unfallen parents have struck him with troubled awe, and the Garden has been recognized to tend, by reason of its exuberance, to wildness. Nevertheless, on the whole there has been little attitudinal uncertainty. When, by exception, darkness is alluded to as pleasant, we sense no rejection of traditional values. The clearest single ambiguity is in the phrase "aspiring Dominations" (III, 392), which historically unoriented readers might conceivably understand to impute praise (but ought not to, since the context is strongly prejudicial). To judge from this evidence only, the epic is anti-sin and pro-virtue; it accepts the common opinion of humanity that flowers are nice, darkness unpleasant, God good, man inclined to be sinful. Milton has, in fact, nothing new in these books to say about values. He does not, like the typical modern writer, attempt to prove that the world's opinions have always been mistaken. His head, moreover, is on the same side as his feelings. What he knows with his heart he also believes with his mind. There is no tension between brain and body, no dissociation of sensibilities. He, and the two books we have been examining, appear from this angle of vision to be all of a piece, untorn by inner contradictions, solid, consistent, harmonious.

Exactly (it may be objected); that is the trouble. The victories are not hard won. Possibly, though, the places to look for internal struggle are Books I, II, IX, X, XI, and XII, rather than III and IV. Yet it might be urged that "integration," of which modern psychology has made a great deal, is not necessarily a worse thing in poetry than in personality, and that there is no really adequate reason to demand that all poems should share our modern diseases.

....

CHAPTER VI

VISUAL

PERCEPTION

In the immediately preceding chapters we have sought in Books I-IV of *Paradise Lost* the affective implications of animistic turns of speech and of two selected rhetorical figures. We turn now to perception—which of course often stimulates affective responses but may be studied in isolation from them —and look first, in Books V and VI, at patterns of seeing.

How hard it is to study visual images objectively will appear from a protracted look at the opening lines of Book V.

> Now Morn her rosie steps in th' Eastern Clime
> Advancing, sowd the Earth with Orient Pearle.

Are visual images present here? and if they are, can readers agree about their content?

The first question is raised by printed comments about imagery, which show disconcerting variations in sensory responses. Apparently some readers see nothing at all in passages which to other readers seem visually rich. About these lines, however, there can be no doubt, for the excerpt is not visually blank. At the very least, the response should include not only an intellectual realization that dawn is coming but also flashes of color, however vague. "Rosie" and "Pearle" are color terms which describe visual phenomena. If the reader does not sense a change in the color of the sky, which is turning red, and in the appearance of the earth, which is being brightened along the eastern horizon, the fault is in him and not in the poetry. How can one "think" red without having a glimpse of redness?

The second question is more troublesome, for it requires us to discriminate between the implicit content of the lines and supplementary images supplied by the reader. Art often stirs the percipient to become creative; indeed, we may find it pleasing because it does. The difference between creative responses, which use the aesthetic work as a point of departure, and re-creative responses, which are characterized by a trustful committing of the mind and the senses to the work, is critically very important; and the latter must be preferred here, since the former make agreement impossible. Care will enable us to separate, in any specific response, the part which is motivated by the art work from the part which has been supplied from our individual resources. The test is the direction in which we are led by an effort to trace the source of the impression. If we move from the impression toward the poem and find in the poem itself justification for every detail of the response, we can be confident that we are writing about the poem. If we must move from the poem toward private associations and personal experiences, the inference will be that we are writing about our minds.

What the poet actually says in the quoted lines is not that dawn came but that Morning, moving her rosy steps forward in the East,[1] threw Orient—Eastern, perhaps with a suggestion of Oriental splendor—pearls over the earth like a sower scattering seed. ("Clime," in its archaic sense of "a region of the earth," has no necessary association with weather.) The basic problem is the degree to which Morning is personified. How vividly, if at all, is the reader called on to attribute human form to her?

---

[1] Or, alternatively, "lifting, raising," if "advance" is to be given the meaning it has in Prospero's "The fringed curtains of thine eye advance," in *The Tempest*, i, ii.

The two most crucial phrases are "rosie steps" and "sowd
. . . with Orient Pearle." "Rosie" can be associated with steps
only if we consent to see rose-colored feet making the steps,
or, alternatively, to see rose-colored pools in the sky as foot-
prints made by invisible feet. Similarly, "sowd the Earth
with Orient Pearle" may inspire us to visualize either a
hand making sweeping movements as it scatters invisible
seed which falls on high points of the earth as patches of
light or to see merely the patches of light, which because
they appear on the earth successively, and without regular
pattern, may be imagined to have been "sown" by an invisible
hand.

Of these choices the latter, in each instance, is more closely
responsible to the lines. Milton does not mention feet, does
not call our attention to a hand. If we perceive them, they are
our perceptions, not the poem's. Moreover, the vision of a
hand and feet might inspire the sketching in of an entire
figure put together from details of mythological paintings
and a private conception of feminine beauty. Anybody with
active senses can easily construct such a figure. Up to a point,
the figure might be determined by contextual demands and
hence not be wholly arbitrary. The hair would be golden and
flowing because the sun is bright and sheds rays. The robe
would be basically Greek because of an inevitable association
with Aurora, but, like the clouds, it would have a soft texture
and would tend to stream, to fade off at the edges. The colors
would be those of the dawn: gold, red or pink, blue, white.
The figure would move not so much toward us as upward,
toward the zenith—with steps, of course, at each of which
a rosy foot and ankle would be revealed, and dipping a hand
into a basket or bag to throw Orient Pearls over the landscape. So far we may seem to be on safe ground; but in fact
the scene Milton described has already been basically falsified,
for the emphasis on pink and pearl implies that the sun, from

which we have borrowed the figure's head, is not yet above the horizon or appears only as a slowly growing disk. If we elaborate the figure still more, by adding (let us say) a fillet of white wool about the brow, a straight Greek nose, and cool gray eyes, the image becomes sharper at the expense of losing contact with the poem. Further, the whole picture will insensibly acquire tonality of some kind, and this again will be a contribution of the reader. Dawn may be dignified, graceful, or seductive as the reader's psychological needs may determine—a goddess coming to bless the earth, a nymph who has had ballet training, a temptress in whose unseen bed Tithon is yawning and stretching after a night of love. In one way or another we please ourselves, flatter our personal desires, create an image which is privately satisfying. What Milton has said, however, is merely that dawn has come, that a rosy flush is spreading in the east and that high points on the horizon are being illuminated. He has included no more details than these because instead of dwelling at length on the visual phenomena of dawn he wanted to hint them and pass on quickly to other poetic business. If we wish to read his poem and not to create one of our own, we should confine our responses to the data he has supplied.

It is in this spirit that imagery will be treated in the present chapter, with reference consistently to visual perceptions that are explicitly or potentially embodied in the verse and with the most rigorous possible exclusion of everything else. The justification, once more, is that our concern is not with Milton's audience but with his epic as a stimulus to response.

The visual impressions embodied in Milton's lines are often general, like those we have looked at, but also frequently rather precise. The general impressions are appropriate to sketch in backgrounds, the more precise ones to give details about the foreground. The following passage, which begins

only three lines further on, will illustrate. Adam wakes from
a light sleep,

> which th' onely sound
> Of leaves and fuming rills, *Aurora's* fan,
> Lightly dispersd, and the shrill Matin Song
> Of Birds on every bough; so much the more
> His wonder was to find unwak'nd *Eve*
> With Tresses discompos'd, and glowing Cheek,
> As through unquiet rest: hee on his side
> Leaning half-rais'd, with looks of cordial Love
> Hung over her enamourd, and beheld
> Beautie, which whether waking or asleep,
> Shot forth peculiar graces; then with voice
> Milde, as when *Zephyrus* on *Flora* breathes,
> Her hand soft touching, whisperd thus. Awake
> My fairest . . .
>
> (v, 5-18)

Here the initial impressions happen to be auditory: rustling
leaves, gurgling water, the shrill morning songs of birds.
"*Aurora's* fan," of which the syntax is very loose, seems not
to be felt but only to scatter the sound of leaves and—apparently—water. The visual images may hold our attention
a little longer.

We are first introduced to Adam's wonder, which is not
visually presented. Eve, whose appearance evokes the wonder,
lies sleeping with discomposed tresses and glowing cheek.
We are to see these details and no others—not her posture
(lying on her back, turned toward Adam, turned away from
him), not her figure, which in that climate and in the absence
of bed clothing must have been fully revealed. Instead of
titillating the reader with piquant observations, Milton focuses
attention where Adam's was focused, on the signs of perturba-

tion in Eve's face and hair. These deserve to be emphasized because they are the first results of Satan's intrusion into Paradise (he has inspired a disturbing dream) and point forward toward the ultimate calamity. Adam's posture is explained rather precisely; and here the point of view shifts back to the reader. Having seen Eve as Adam sees her, we move back slightly to see the couple in a stage tableau. He leans "half-rais'd"—surely on one elbow—"with looks of cordial Love" as he hangs over her enamored. What attracts him is "Beautie, which whether waking or asleep,/ Shot forth peculiar graces." He is contemplating not her body but—presumably—her face, framed in disorderly hair. He speaks to Eve mildly (an acoustic notation which implies the softness of his mood), touches her hand by moving his free arm, and whispers, "Awake . . ."

Although Milton has many descriptive techniques, that used here is not untypical. That the little scene is rather sharply visual is clear from the fact that it could easily be painted. To be sure, most painters, whether of an earlier century or of our own, would include details that Milton has omitted: for example, complete bodies. What is really called for, however, is a picture in close focus. Eve's head would be in the foreground; Adam's upper body would hang over it; in the background, indistinctly seen, would be leaves, rivulets, and birds. The heads and Adam's chest and arms would be painted to accord with the descriptions given in Book IV, 288-324. The reader, too, from his memories of that book can supply wanton gold ringlets, fair large front, hyacinthine locks, female softness, and male sublimity. We are not, of course, to infer that Milton shies away Puritanically from naked bodies. In the earlier passage, he described them with enough gusto to suggest that he himself was a frustrated nudist. At this point he does not want whole bodies because

109

his interest is in psychological states, and these can best be described in terms of faces and Adam's raised trunk.

We dare continue through only one additional passage before abandoning line-by-line scrutiny for a more synoptic discussion, though of course we shall sometimes linger over samples.

> the morning shines, and the fresh field
> Calls us; we lose the prime, to mark how spring
> Our tended Plants, how blows the Citron Grove,
> What drops the Myrrhe, and what the balmie Reed,
> How Nature paints her colours, how the Bee
> Sits on the Bloom extracting liquid sweet.
> Such whispering wak'd her, but with startl'd eye
> On *Adam*, whom imbracing, thus she spake.
>
> (v, 20-27)

The focus has been again diffused and again sharpened, as if Milton had worked with a zoom lens which he shot forward for a close-up, retracted, and then advanced a second time. The Garden is presented in a series of quick flashes that offer chiefly motor imagery: the plants spring, the citron grove blows or blossoms, the myrrh and reed drop gum and balm, nature paints, the bee extracts. Apart from the pervasive shining of morning, the visual hints appeal to whatever general memories the reader may have of flower beds, citrus orchards, gum trees and reeds, a profusion of natural color, and bees sucking on flowers. Once more it would be a mistake for the reader to see more than the poetry describes. To use the cinematographic analogy again, the visual screen should offer successive images with blurred edges, the whole series occupying no more time than it takes to read the words. We are not expected really to see the lush Garden setting but only to understand, and perhaps in some degree empathetically to share, Adam's eagerness to be up and about in it. Energetic growth is emphasized because Adam feels the growth as a pressure. At the end we see Eve awakening with startled eye and at once embracing him, as if to gain support. The lens has again moved forward for a close-up first of eyes and then of upper bodies.

We must not, therefore, expect to find one kind of image only but a number of different kinds, each chosen for a specific purpose. The temptation to say "This is how Milton saw" must be resisted, for he saw in many ways, depending on local context and the variations in his narrative purpose. Nonetheless we may make a rough preliminary distinction between general and precise images and examine first a number of the former, taking care to draw appropriate distinctions.

The following lines are about as general as description can be. Eve is quoting the voice which spoke to her in her dream.

> now reignes
> Full Orbd the Moon, and with more pleasing light
> Shadowie sets off the face of things; in vain,
> If none regard; Heav'n wakes with all his eyes.
>
> (v, 41-44)

We glimpse a full moon which dominates the sky ("reignes") and illuminates parts of the landscape while leaving other parts in deep shadow, and we see multitudes of stars ("Heav'n wakes with all his eyes"). Nothing more. Although we know the nature of the landscape from earlier descriptions, a proper illustration would be brushed in very sketchily except for the sky, which because of its brilliance pulls the eye upwards. Nothing could be more suitable, for the "gentle voice" of the Tempter, speaking to Eve in a dream, proceeds to say, "Whom to behold but thee, Natures desire?" Satan's purpose is not to evoke gratitude for God's gifts of tree and bush and field but to flatter, and this he can do by pretending that Heaven's waking is caused by admiration of Eve. The mention of pleasing shadows is preparatory. He wants Eve to get up, to come out of the bower, and he must suggest that something pleasant is there for her to see. He does not, however, really want her to look, for he intends to fill her mind with thoughts of disobedience to God, and this he cannot do if her attention is drawn to "the face of things." Once outside the bower, he can hope that she will glance momentarily at the heavens and then begin immediately to put herself at the center of all creation, to imagine herself a cynosure ("all things joy, with ravishment/ Attracted by thy beauty still to gaze," v, 46-47). That the stratagem is clever is shown by its complete success within the limits of the dream. Abstract as the description is, it is right for its situation.

So often. We may look at other examples.

> Forthwith up to the Clouds
> With him I flew, and underneath beheld
> The Earth outstretcht immense, a prospect wide
> And various.
>
> (v, 86-89)

Clouds, an immense panorama of variegated landscape: Eve has an indistinct view because she is thinking about herself ("wondring at my flight and change/ To this high exaltation," v, 89-90). A clearer image would falsify her state of mind, which must be what it is because she is dreaming of sin. Throughout *Paradise Lost* sin is fundamentally pride, the placing of oneself at the center—exactly what Eve is doing now.

> But first from under shadie arborous roof
> Soon as they forth were come to op'n sight
> Of day-spring, and the Sun, who scarce up risen
> With wheels yet hov'ring ore the Ocean brim,

> Shot paralel to the Earth his dewie ray,
> Discovering in wide Lantskip all the East
> Of Paradise and *Edens* happie Plains . . .
>
> (v, 137-43)

This might be introductory to another set-piece of the kind
we were given in Book IV, and it is beautifully managed. The
description is not developed, however, because our attention
is to fall on Adam and Eve: "Lowly they bowd adoring, and
began/ Thir Orisons . . ." (v, 144-45). We are to hear the
prayer rather than to watch the natural spectacle which inspires gratitude toward the Divine Giver.

> wave your tops, ye Pines,
> With every Plant, in sign of Worship wave.
>
> (v, 193-94)

A glimpse of treetops in motion, but only a glimpse, for the
prayer must attain scope by enumeration and cannot pause
long upon details of the "universal Frame," however "wondrous fair" (v, 154-55) the Parents find it. At most, the poet
can afford now and then just enough elaboration to suggest
that the catalogue is kept spare by deliberate suppression of
much that is deeply appreciated, as in an immediately preceding passage:

> Ye Mists and Exhalations that now rise
> From Hill or steaming Lake, duskie or grey,
> Till the Sun paint your fleecie skirts with Gold,
> In honour to the Worlds great Author rise,
> Whether to deck with Clouds th' uncolourd skie,
> Or wet the thirstie Earth with falling showers.
>
> (v, 185-90)

For the most part, the appropriate technique is that of sugges-
tive allusion: "ye Birds,/ That singing up to Heaven Gate

ascend . . . " (v, 197-98); "Yee that in Waters glide, and yee that walk/ The Earth, and stately tread, or lowly creep" (v, 200-201); "Hill, or Valley, Fountain or fresh shade" (v, 203). Although Milton was blind, to accuse him of ocular insensitivity because he does not painstakingly develop visual images at times when he is performing other kinds of poetic business would be otiose. An epic poem requires the use of many techniques, not one only, and the choice of one often temporarily involves the rejection of others.

No doubt some of the excerpts just quoted will appear to many readers not to have any visual quality at all. "Wave your tops, ye Pines": do we—or, better, should we—see anything as we read the words? This is an extreme instance, and by discussing it we can avoid considering the others. We should have, I think, briefly and without sharp edges, but not *vaguely*, an image of massed green pinetops agitated voluntarily, as it were, and not because they are blown by the wind. What can "wave" mean except to swing visibly back and forth, and what can the tops of pines be except branches covered with pine needles and therefore green? The massing of the trees may be a private contribution to the image, produced by innumerable vistas of pine forests; but it is probably both more natural and easier than darting glimpses of isolated trees. That the waving is voluntary, metaphorically speaking, is clear from the syntactical form: "Wave your tops!" If forced to explicate, we say, of course, that in fact the tops are moved by the wind, but that Adam and Eve interpret the motion as an expression of a worshipful attitude in the trees themselves. A reader who does not react to the passage in some such way as has been described does not, I think, submit himself fully to the poetry, does not allow it to determine the forms of his consciousness. (It goes without saying that someone who does not see poetry well may hear it or think it superbly; but at the moment we are concerned only with visual perceptions.) The only alternative reading that would not be less rich is one in which the dimness of the visual image is compensated for by abnormal kinaesthetic empathy: a faint sense of muscular strain replaces a vision on the retina of the imagination. I suspect, however, that this would be rare.

We pass on next to sharper and more elaborately developed images, again proceeding straight on through Book V instead of returning to pick up passages we have missed. One appears in the next verse paragraph.

> On to thir mornings rural work they haste
> Among sweet dewes and flours; where any row
> Of Fruit-trees overwoodie reachd too farr
> Thir pamperd boughes, and needed hands to check
> Fruitless imbraces: or they led the Vine
> To wed her Elm; she spous'd about him twines
> Her mariageable arms, and with her brings
> Her dowr th' adopted Clusters, to adorn
> His barren leaves. Them thus imploid beheld
> With pittie Heav'ns high King . . .
>
> (v, 211-20)

In the first line we follow Adam and Eve to the scene of their labors; at the end God looks down at them, pityingly. In between we watch them at their work, seeing, however, rather what they do than them doing it.

The descriptive method here, as elsewhere, is not realistic, does not aim at acquainting the reader with precise details of space and shape and size and peculiarity. Such as they are, the specifications are generic. Milton is intent on the norm, the archetype, rather than on variations from it. The world he portrays is still unfallen; the elm has been blasted by no thunderstorms, the flowers have been visited by no blight. There is as yet no real individuality in the world either of nature or of men. Accordingly, critics who think that description must concentrate on the idiosyncratic qualities of objects are likely to be disappointed. "Don't show us a Tree; show us *this tree*": The advice is sound enough for our own time, when the sphere of art has come to be thought of as that of the specific, but it is irrelevant to most pre-Romantic literature and especially irrelevant to Milton, who took seriously an aesthetic that originated with Aristotle and by the High Renaissance had become not only official but unquestionable. Even writers like Donne and Marvell, whose aesthetic practices more nearly resemble our own, probably would have granted the principles in theory.

The Happy Pair work "among sweet dewes and flours," occupying themselves especially "where any row/ Of Fruit-trees overwoodie reachd too farr/ Thir pamperd boughes," lopping branches to relieve "Fruitless imbraces"; or "they led the Vine/ To wed her Elm," twining her "mariageable arms" about the trunk so that she might bring "Her dowr th' adopted Clusters, to adorn/ His barren leaves." The images are not static but move, shift with the gardeners' activities. The gardeners themselves are invisible, kept out of sight by a fine tact. We see, at most, working hands and perhaps arms. A suspicion may arise that the vine's arms are borrowed from a subliminal glimpse of the lovely arms of Eve. By intention, however, Milton keeps Eve's beauty out of the picture in order to show us the Parents doing what the terms of the poem require us to wish them to do indefinitely. The tonality of the description is that of connubial love: pampering, embraces, a wedding, a "spous'd" vine clasping a tree trunk animistically with marriageable arms, a dowry, and, at the end, a suggestion that grapes borne by the vine will compensate for the barrenness of the elm. The spiritual ("pamperd") and physical love of the happy couple spreads into the Garden in which they labor; and the consequence is that we are made to feel somewhat more intimately the idyllic quality of a situation which later will be corrupted by sin.

The sharper and more elaborately developed images (as I have called them) are thus frequently generic and differ from the "general" ones noted earlier mainly in being dwelt on longer. When Raphael, on his visit to Eden, alights "on th' Eastern cliff of Paradise" (v, 275), he is described in terms which might have suited equally well any other seraph:

> six wings he wore, to shade
> His lineaments Divine; the pair that clad
> Each shoulder broad, came mantling ore his brest
> With regal Ornament; the middle pair
> Girt like a Starrie Zone his waste, and round
> Skirted his loines and thighes with downie Gold
> And colours dipt in Heav'n; the third his feet
> Shaddowd from either heele with featherd maile
> Skie-tinctur'd grain. Like *Maia's* son he stood,
> And shook his Plumes, that Heav'nly fragrance filld
> The circuit wide. Strait knew him all the Bands
> Of Angels under watch . . .
>
> (v, 277-88)

The passage is a development of the description of a seraph in *Isaiah* (6:2) and except for the shaking of the plumes to put them in order after the long flight from Heaven—an attractive detail, which not only generates a flurry of color but also suggests that Milton had watched birds attentively and *felt* the flight as flight—in no way differentiates Raphael from any other angel in his order. That there are in fact differences among angels is made adequately clear further on, when Abdiel contrasts strikingly with the rebellious angels and later achieves individuality within his own group. Again, Michael, in Books XI and XII, attains distinctness from Raphael by reason of greater austerity: he wears a sword and carries a spear, when greeted by a bow "hee Kingly from his State/ Inclin'd not" (XI, 249-50), and in other ways he is made to appear more business-like and less genial. In both these instances, however, individualization occurs within a context of disobedience. When we meet Raphael the sublunary world is still ordered, still harmonious; and in such a world individuals approximate archetypes. Idiosyncrasy results usually from movements of the will which deny the natural order of values and consequently gradually modify not only character but even appearance—as Satan is marked by the care which sits on his faded cheek (I, 601-602). Before the Fall the human pair and their whole universe of experience must be described, however sketchily or exhaustively, in terms of species, and the details must be those appropriate to the order to which the individual belongs.

Such, in broad patterns, are the two dominant types of visual imagery in the parts of *Paradise Lost* which have to do with the unfallen world: more and less fully developed descriptions of archetypal beings and objects, the degree of elaboration depending, quite sensibly, on the nature of the poetic business in hand. The poet's own visual sense is always active, but he does not allow himself to paint rich word pictures when the aesthetic economy of his poem requires that the emphasis fall on something else. *Ut pictura poësis*, Horace had said; well enough, but epic had been shown by Homer and Virgil—not to mention their Renaissance Italian imitators—to deserve no less than tragedy definition as an "imitation of an action," and this particular series of actions, because it was intended to justify God's ways to men, demanded that special care be given to rational explication, to the analysis of mental states, and to other matters not pictorial in quality and not requiring pictorial presentation except on the basis of a doctrinaire aesthetic held neither by Milton nor by his contemporary readers. Moreover, the very hugeness of Milton's intention required that his poem move steadily forward. Donne's example is instructive here; his *Progresse of the Soule* (the attempt at an epic, not the second *Anniversarie* poem) aborted because of a fatal tendency to stare at its own tracks. Donne was incapable of glancing at anything. His gaze either skipped over or became fixed. Milton, in contrast, could stride along briskly between incidents, noticing colors and forms by which he did not allow himself to become hypnotized. His descriptive methods differed, however, when he treated fallen personages, for a will alienated from God no longer accepted the universal order but strove for individuation. Although the most brilliant and detailed dramatization of self-will appears in Books IX-XII, Book VI contains a preliminary sketch of revolt on the angelic level. To it, therefore, we now turn in the hope that a look at a relatively unsuccessful part of the epic will be instructive.

Visual imagery in the War in Heaven is affected by the unsuitability of the metaphor to the semantic burden. The easiest, and perhaps also the truest, explanation of the failure in poetic tact would be that Milton's respect for ancient example induced a resigned acceptance of precedent.

> Not sedulous by Nature to indite
> Warrs, hitherto the onely Argument
> Heroic deemd, chief maistrie to dissect
> With long and tedious havoc fabl'd Knights
> In Battels feignd . . .
>
> (ix, 27-31)

The honesty of the delayed confession wins our respect; but except at the end, where the poet's imagination caught fire, Book VI shows, alternatively, boredom and strain, from which relief is sought in heavy irony.

The strain shows itself in inconsistencies and self-contradictions, rare elsewhere but surprisingly numerous here. Some of these are nonvisual in quality; for example, Satan's remark to Beëlzebub, after he has begun on the night following the Son's elevation to infuse bad influence into that unwary breast, that "More in this place/ To utter is not safe" (v, 682-83). Satan ought not to be unaware of God's omniscience, nor ought knowledge of the omniscience to be so badly disseminated in Heaven that Satan can expect Beëlzebub to be unaware of it. We dislike the thought of a tricky God. Again we are disturbed when we read that on the first day of the war not only Satan, but all the bad angels, "weend/ That self same day by fight, or by surprize/ To win the Mount of God" (vi, 86-88). Evidently God's omnipotence has been as carefully concealed as His omniscience. Once more, the Son's creation of all the angels—the act which, up to this point, has most unmistakably demonstrated not only His power but also His special relationship to the Father—is apparently not known, or so indistinctly known that Satan can risk lying publicly about it.

> That we were formd then saist thou? and the work
> Of secondarie hands, by task transferrd
> From Father to his Son? strange point and new!
>
> (v, 853-55)

We should have preferred that God and the Son had dealt openly enough with their followers to make the rebellion quite clearly a result of poisoned wills. As things stand, the inference is that the rebels are inadequately informed about the hierarchy which should determine their allegiances.

Other inconsistencies have a visual aspect, although this is often so subdued as not to be immediately apparent. The advance of the good angels into battle will furnish a convenient starting point:

> nor obvious Hill,
> Nor streit'ning Vale, nor Wood, nor Stream divides

Thir perfet ranks; for high above the ground
Thir march was, and the passive Air upbore
Thir nimble tread.

(VI, 69-73)

Memories of Homeric and Virgilian battles are combined
here with a realization that angels are not earthbound like
human beings. The result, no doubt partly intentional, is
grotesque. If Milton wants his angels to fly, well and good;
we welcome the gesture toward verisimilitude. "March," however, is too obvious and easy a compromise because it results
from the slightest possible modification of the classic models
and shows no real effort to adapt the tradition to novel conditions. Moreover, these are Michael's hosts, not Satan's, and
they ought not to appear stupid. Even apart from these con-
siderations the image is unsatisfactory; we can sense so vividly that we can almost see the lack of purchase for the angelic
feet. Yet ineffectual as the mode of advance is, it is presented
as a minor triumph of military tactics—"Nor streit'ning Vale,
nor Wood, nor Stream divides/ Thir perfect ranks."

This inauspicious beginning leads immediately to further
complications. The angels have appeared to be walking at
something like a normal military pace or at most are moving
at quick-time. We have not been encouraged to see them as
taking thousand-mile steps, and they certainly are not flying
("Thir nimble tread"). At such a pace they nevertheless
progress, in no time at all, "over many a tract/ Of Heav'n
. . . many a Province wide/ Tenfold the length of this
terrene" (VI, 76-78). The reader's best choice is to accept the
statement as idea in order not to force an adjustment of his
already-formed image to it; he lets the troops go on march-
ing as before while an invisible landscape changes beneath
them. The alternatives are to imagine a kind of step which will
carry over huge distances angels of a size proportionate to the

Heavenly landscape or suddenly to expand the warriors' size sufficiently to dwarf the Heaven they inhabit. Since either transformation is awkward and both commit us to the correction of an image derived legitimately from the preceding description, we simply refuse to entertain the tracts and provinces as visual entities and accept them as mere concepts.

To meet this host comes another from the opposite direction, bristling

> with upright beams innumerable
> Of rigid Spears, and Helmets throngd, and Shields
> Various, with boastful Argument portraid,
> The banded Powers of *Satan* hasting on
> With furious expedition.
>
> (vi, 82-86)

We are brought back to the Homeric or Virgilian image and, when we hear that "the shout/ Of Battel now began, and rushing sound/ Of onset" (vi, 96-98), we expect next to be offered glimpses of general and individual combat—differing, of course, in that the warring bands are in the air instead of on solid ground, but evidently in other respects not basically unclassical. Satan, we read, sat in his sun-bright chariot "High in the midst exalted as a God" (vi, 99), and we infer that as leader he has taken his station higher in the air than his followers. From the ground we look up at massed millions of heavily armed warriors rushing weightlessly toward each other in the sky. But no: the poet has changed his mind about "Battel" and "onset" and causes Satan to "light"—we understand the meaning to be "alight"—from his "gorgeous Throne" (vi, 103),

> for now
> 'Twixt Host and Host but narrow space was left,

A dreadful interval, and Front to Front
Presented stood in terrible array.

(VI, 103-106)

Are the armies now on the ground? It would seem so, for we learn immediately that "*Satan* with vast and hautie strides advanc't" (VI, 109). Conceivably, however, Satan walks on air as the advancing good angels had done. We are left uncertain and balance between the two possibilities, viewing the scene in one way and then scrambling it to recompose it in the other.

There follows a meditation of Abdiel, after which, "Forth stepping opposite, half way he met/ His daring foe" (VI, 128-29), whether in air or on the ground is not specified. In the succeeding exchange of taunts with Satan there is little visual imagery except of a glancing kind. Abdiel mentions the Omnipotent's "solitarie hand," which "Reaching beyond all limit, at one blow/ Unaided could have finisht thee" (VI, 139-41); Satan, "with scornful eye askance" (VI, 149), replies; and single words such as "Synod," "Plume," "Feast," "path," "Hell," "Heav'n," and "Chains" (VI, 156-86) might conceivably evoke images in an excited mind. Words now give place to overt action which includes gesture and movement.

So saying, a noble stroke he lifted high,
Which hung not, but so swift with tempest fell
On the proud Crest of *Satan*, that no sight,
Nor motion of swift thought, less could his Shield
Such ruin intercept: ten paces huge
He back recoild; the tenth on bended knee
His massie Spear upstaid.

(VI, 189-95)

Since we find special difficulty in visualizing the butt of the spear as a support in the air, we conclude that from the beginning we should have imaged the confrontation as occur-

123

ring on the ground. One may be pardoned, however, for feeling that Milton should have informed us and for suspecting that he himself did not see clearly the actions he undertook to describe.

Other problems arise as we read on. Sometimes the image is clear enough as an image but awakens discomfort because it has troublesome implications. The following passage will illustrate:

> led in fight, yet Leader seemd
> Each Warriour single as in Chief, expert
> When to advance, or stand, or turn the sway
> Of Battel, op'n when, and when to close
> The ridges of grim Warr.
>
> (vi, 232-36)

The picture here is of the kind I have described as "general" in that it offers only hurried and incomplete images of skilled soldiers advancing, holding their ground, turning disadvantage into advantage, opening ranks to let a charge pass harmlessly through, and closing ranks when doing so will oppose a stronger force to a weaker one. If the sensations of movement are stronger than those of line and color, we nevertheless know enough by now about the appearance of the combatants to glimpse the figures that move. What is awkward is the impropriety of the images to the poem. Since there has never previously been war in Heaven, the implication is that the angels, through uncounted millennia, have been trained like the Parliamentary militia of Civil War England in spite of the fact that no external enemy was in sight and that when an internal one arose the training would benefit rebels quite as much as loyalists. Conceivably Milton intends us to believe that because the angels are supernal beings they are supernally good even at warfare, which they understand by intuitive knowledge (cf. v, 486-89), but we again suspect the indolent acceptance of an inappropriate tradition. Or take the "fierie foaming Steeds" which by VI, 391, lie overturned with the chariots. Are they "real" horses which have existed for a long time in Heaven (having been created for use in martial drills), been broken and trained like earthly horses and turned out to pasture between times? Or have they, perhaps, been conjured up instantaneously, as Satan has produced a coronet and silver wand for his interview with Uriel (III, 640 and 644) and a spear and shield for his earthly encounter with Gabriel (IV, 989-90)? If the steeds have been produced by magic, we are at a loss to say why cannon—which, after all, even fallen man can manufacture—require a night's industrial activity to produce. The other furniture of war—the chariots, the armor used to cover bodies which when sliced in two reunite quickly, the shields—raises similar questions, provokes a similar uneasiness. We are troubled, also by the "grateful truce" imposed by darkness (VI, 406-407) because we were told earlier that darkness in Heaven is like mere twilight on earth (VI, 11-12) and have just been informed that the good angels, at least, in fight "stood/ Unwearied" (VI, 403-404). Terrestrial battles cease at nightfall because of exhaustion and real darkness. The cessation of hostilities in Heaven resembles the ritual stopping of a cricket match for tea.

These criticisms are not met by the assertion that the War is wholly ironic or that, as Arnold Stein has suggested, the entire episode is comedy on such a stupendous scale that we do not laugh at it. Undoubtedly Book VI is full of grim humor, but the humor often does not *take*, for it seems to have been necessitated by an error in poetic strategy. The notion of "accommodation" is itself unexceptionable:

> what surmounts the reach
> Of human sense, I shall delineat so,

By lik'ning spiritual to corporeal forms.

(v, 571-73)

What causes resistance is the choice of these forms, this Homeric metaphor. Because the metaphor falsifies roles, imputes wrong motives, carries implications irrelevant or contradictory to the intended meanings, and by its nature generates grotesqueries which the poet himself is unwilling or unable to resolve, it is the wrong metaphor for Milton's purpose. Elsewhere *Paradise Lost* is almost invulnerable to any criticism except that which refuses to grant the epic's preassumptions. In the War Milton undercuts his own ground, presumably because of a half-bored acceptance of epic tradition. Picking faults in a masterpiece which I myself not only think but feel to be the highest achievement of English nondramatic poetry is an ungrateful task; but doing so has provided me with an opportunity to suggest that we wrong the poem if we do not measure it against the highest possible standards. We do not truly honor a literary work if we view it through a fog of admiration, for then we fail to see not only its weaknesses but also its real merits.

Of course the War is not all feebly imagined. Milton, after all, is Milton, and his slumbers are more perceptive than much wakefulness. But he does not always slumber even in this uncongenial task. The meeting of Michael and Satan is vividly imagined in a vein similar to that of the player's recitation to Hamlet about the destruction of Troy.

Now wav'd thir fierie Swords, and in the Aire
Made horrid Circles; two broad Suns thir Shields
Blaz'd opposite, while expectation stood
In horror; from each hand with speed retir'd
Where erst was thickest fight, th' Angelic throng,
And left large field, unsafe within the wind

Of such commotion, such as to set forth
Great things by small, if Natures concord broke,
Among the Constellations warr were sprung,
Two Planets rushing from aspect maligne
Of fiercest opposition in mid Skie,
Should combat, and thir jarring Sphears confound . . .

(VI, 304-15)

The image of heroic warriors waving bright swords which
cause bystanders to flee to a safe distance modulates, by means
of the *topos* beginning *magna parvis conferre*, into a description of gigantic catastrophe in the heavens—a simile which is
made doubly effective by our realization, first, that the planets
to whom the warriors are compared are small when measured
against the archangels and, secondly, that the archangels are
themselves, almost literally, Heavenly bodies. "Aspect maligne"
is both an astrological phrase and a description of facial expressions. The sword-play which follows has an adequately
clear visual pattern; Michael's sword "met"

The sword of *Satan* with steep force to smite
Descending, and in half cut sheere, nor staid,
But with swift wheele reverse, deep entring shar'd
All his right side; then *Satan* first knew pain,
And writh'd him to and fro convolv'd; so sore
The griding sword with discontinuous wound
Passd through him . . .

(VI, 324-30)

If the explanation that "th' Ethereal substance clos'd/ Not
long divisible" (330-31) somewhat chills our affective partici-
pation in the contest, the situation is partly retrieved by the
account of how Satan was borne on shields back to his chariot,
where he lay "Gnashing for anguish and despite and shame"
(VI, 340). Not all the details are visual—unlike a critic, who

chooses limited perspectives for the attainment of specific
ends, the poet does not specialize in one kind of imagery at
one time—but the effect, on the whole, is satisfactory. If
the War were described everywhere in terms like these, we
would say that the "port" of "gigantick loftiness" noted by
Johnson fitted Milton well for the writing of Book VI.

There are other successes and other failures. We come upon
sharply-limned pictures which are the more effective for
leaving the imagination some play:

> in th' assembly next upstood
> *Nisroc*, of Principalities the prime;
> As one he stood escap't from cruel fight,
> Sore toild, his riven Armes to havoc hewn,
> And cloudie in aspect.
>
> (VI, 446-50)

> others from the dawning Hills
> Lookd round, and Scouts each Coast light-armed scoure,
> Each quarter, to descrie the distant foe.
>
> (VI, 528-30)

The description of the completed cannon (VI, 569-80), whatever one may think of Milton's desire to condemn such
weapons of destruction by assigning their invention to devils,
is visually precise. On the other side, the "jaculation dire"
(VI, 665) of hills which so fill the air that "under ground"
the competing hosts "fought in dismal shade" (VI, 666) is
less impressive than outrageous—an adaptation, this time, of
the War of the Titans mentioned by Hesiod, and visually
disruptive because in order to see it at all one must either expand the angels' stature to the point where the Heavenly
landscape seems quite unsuitable for them or else try to
imagine tiny, Herculean figures manipulating, as if they were
clumps of dirt, mountains beneath which they would be

nearly invisible and whose tops they could not have reached. Further, nothing is made of the rivers and lakes the poet himself has mentioned: "the seated Hills with all thir load,/ Rocks, Waters, Woods"—(vi, 644-45). Having thought of these, he immediately forgets them and is unaware of the torrents which, once the hills were turned upside down, would have streamed down upon jaculating angels and the broken ground. Grimly he works out some of the gross implications of his derivative idea without bothering to perceive the situation clearly. Here picture is subordinated to concept as carelessly as anywhere in the whole enormous work.

At this point a transformation occurs; the poet himself becomes engrossed, and to the end of the book failures of vision are overwhelmed by authentic elevation and a breathtaking rush. The failures, which may claim our notice first, are likely to appear only on close reading. (I am not aware that attention has ever been called to them.) What, for instance, has happened to the second night? When our gaze is drawn from the "horrid confusion heapt/ Upon confusion" (vi, 668-69) of the battle to God, "Shrin'd in his Sanctuarie of Heav'n secure" (vi, 672), we still seem to be in the morning of the second day. All that has happened is that the armies have met, the cannon have been revealed and have spoken, and the good angels have retaliated by throwing hills. After a speech by the Father and a reply by the Son, we read,

> he ore his Scepter bowing, rose
> From the right hand of Glorie where he sate,
> And the third sacred Morn began to shine
> Dawning through Heav'n.
>
> (vi, 746-49)

The best way to handle the temporal lapse is probably to ignore it. An effort to account for it draws our attention distractingly from the poem and is no more likely to succeed than an attempt to resolve the famous problem of the two times in *Othello*. Again, we picture the "Quiver with three-bolted Thunder stor'd" (VI, 764) before we learn that it must have contained the "ten thousand Thunders" mentioned later (VI, 836). Since we had had no idea that it was so capacious, we must go back and revise the image. In line 840 the Son rides "Ore Shields and Helmes, and helmed heads"; in line 858 we are told that he drove "them"—apparently all the rebels—"before him Thunder-strook" toward the crystal wall. True, it is said that "the overthrown he rais'd, and as a Herd/ Of Goats or timerous flock together throngd" (VI, 856-57) swept them before His chariot; but we are nonetheless forced somehow to gather up and hurry in front of the wheels combatants over whom they had passed. One wonders, too, about the "branching Palme" by which "each order bright" is shaded as it advances to meet the Sole Victor when He turns His chariot (VI, 880-86). The orders, or as many members of them as had participated in the War, had been armed only moments earlier ("here stand/ Ye Angels armd"—VI, 801-802). The situation is complicated by the fact that the Son came "Attended with ten thousand thousand Saints" (VI, 767) who presumably had not participated in the fighting, but "all his Saints," of line 882, must surely have included the fighters also. Where did the palms come from, and what has happened to the weapons and armor if, as the suggestion of Palm Sunday perhaps illegitimately hints, we cannot help visualizing white robes? The easiest solution is simply to replace one image by another without trying to effect a transition.

All this, however, is mere fault-picking. In the main, the passage makes us helpless by its brilliance and energy. The large-scale architectonics of the action is admirably clear. Rising from his throne next to the Father, the Son mounts His chariot (to which we shall return in a moment) and proceeds to the battlefield flanked by ten million saints and

twenty thousand other chariots. As He progresses, the up-
rooted hills and disordered landscape, by a process with which
modern readers have been familiarized by seeing motion pictures run backwards, resumes its former pleasantness:

> At his command th' uprooted Hills retir'd
> Each to his place, they heard his voice and went
> Obsequious, Heav'n his wonted face renewd,
> And with fresh Flourets Hill and Valley smil'd.
> (VI, 781-84)

Already the good angels have been induced by the unexpected apparition of the Son to fall back, "circumfus'd on
either Wing" (VI, 778) , whereas the rebels "Took envie, and
aspiring to his highth,/ Stood reimbatteld fierce" (VI, 793-94).
Except for the ten million noncombatant saints and the
twenty thousand chariots, who apparently continue to be
abreast of the Son when His chariot halts, the arrangement
offers no visual difficulty. We can even orient the scene by the
compass if we choose, for we know that the rebels have come
southward from Satan's realms in the north (V, 689). The Son,
having instructed the bright array of saints to desist from their
efforts, changes His countenance into terror and drives forward with irresistible force, throwing His thunders while
the four cherubim who draw His chariot and also the eyes
with which the wheels are set (a bold stroke that inspires us
to identify the missiles with glances) shower arrows. The
chariot drives straight forward over prostrate bodies, which
are then raised and, along with the rebels who have escaped
being crushed, are swept to the crystal wall of Heaven, which
opens to let them pass. Those who are swept through the
breach and those who throw themselves headlong through it
(VI, 864) tumble through Chaos, to which our gaze turns
next; we hear Chaos roar with anger while his realm is
"incumberd" with falling ("ruin," VI, 874); Hell finally

"Yawning receavd them whole, and on them clos'd" (VI, 875); the crystal wall restores itself, the Son turns His chariot and rides amidst singing hosts to "the Courts/ And Temple of his mightie Father" (889-90), where He resumes His seat and now still sits in glory.

It is an astonishing and unforgettable picture. Through it all we watch the unbelievable and yet somehow acceptable chariot (which seems right because we recognize echoes from *Ezekiel*):

> Flashing thick flames, Wheele within Wheele undrawn,
> It self instinct with Spirit, but convoyd
> By four Cherubic shapes, four Faces each
> Had wondrous, as with Starrs thir bodies all
> And Wings were set with Eyes, with Eyes the Wheels
> Of Beril, and careering Fires between;
> Over thir heads a crystal Firmament,
> Whereon a Saphir Throne, inlaid with pure
> Amber, and colours of the showrie Arch.
>
> (VI, 751-59)

The irrelevant Homer—or, more precisely, Virgil—has been abandoned for a more authoritative, less humanly limited source, and the poet himself has taken wings. He has had no real taste for sword-play, but the triumph of good over evil causes him to vibrate in every fiber of both mind and body. The effectiveness results, of course, from magnificent sound and motor imagery as well as from visual effects, and these the limitation of our view does not permit us to consider. The crescendo, however, is so great, the power so much beyond our ability to resist, that as we turn the page to begin Book VII we can forgive the perfunctoriness of the descriptions through which the poet accumulated the resources from which he has produced this climax.

....

CHAPTER VII

AUDITORY

PERCEPTION

Book VII of *Paradise Lost* is given over wholly to a description of the six days of creation. Book VIII begins with a discussion of astronomy, continues with Adam's story of his earliest memories—his awakening to consciousness, his colloquy with the divine shape that appears from among the trees, the creation of Eve and the joy of their first meeting—and concludes with a dialogue on love, initiated by Adam's rather excessive praise of Eve and terminated by Raphael's comments about love among the angels. Book VII is mostly visual—a stupendous, ocular panorama of the successive stages of creation. Book VIII is dialogue. Adam's reflections imply a problem; Raphael discusses it, and the conversation thereafter is partly descriptive, partly argumentative, and partly hortatory. Except at the end of Book VII, where the returning Son is acclaimed by hymns and instrumental music, neither book offers any special opportunity for a heavy concentration of sound images. In the unfallen world of Book VII, the discordant clamor of Books I and II, or again of the War in Heaven, is excluded; and the emerging universe does not yet sing to its Maker, as in Book IV. Book VIII is mostly quiet talk. Under the circumstances, the intention to consider auditory images may appear very odd.

Nowhere, perhaps, will the approach basic to the present study be put to a more severe test. I assume, however, that a phenomenon can sometimes be examined advantageously at the point of least density as well as at the point of greatest. The choice depends on whether one's interest is in what is pervasive or in what is exceptional. The usual practice, in discussing Milton's style, has been to study peaks. Doing so helps us to understand what the poet can do at his best, but it may also create misconceptions about what he does characteristically. The worst generalizations about his epic style, probably, have been those which depended on a half-dozen virtuoso passages scrutinized intensively. My purpose here is the contrary, but equally legitimate, one of looking at the ground from which the peaks rise; and the method of doing so is to study successive two-book sections of the poem without special reference to their subject matter.

A note must be added about what is meant by "auditory awareness." As used here, the phrase does not suggest merely a sensitivity to the auditory aspects of actions or events or objects which are a part of the poetic subject matter; for example, the clash of steel on steel in war, the hymning of angels, the bubbling of a stream. It means rather consciousness of acoustic data of all kinds, and not least of the sound of the poetry itself. In some of the remarks that follow onomatopoeic effects will be noted—the imitation by the verse itself of sounds mentioned in it or implied by it. Elsewhere the emphasis will be on the creation, in the poetry, of acoustic effects which are metaphorical equivalents of meanings. Instead of explaining the last sentence fully here, I shall hope that it will become clear as the discussion proceeds.

Book VII opens with an invocation to Urania, "whose Voice divine/ Following" (2-3) the poet will soar above the Olympian Hill and the flight of Pegasean wing. He calls "The meaning, not the Name" (5), but he does so by pronouncing the name; and he further associates Urania with sound by describing her as "conversing" songfully with her sister

Wisdom in the presence of God, who was pleased by what He heard.

> Thou with Eternal wisdom didst converse,
> Wisdom thy Sister, and with her didst play
> In presence of th' Almightie Father, pleas'd
> With thy Celestial Song.
>
> (VII, 9-12)

Half of the poet's song yet remains unsung (21), but he now sings more confidently, "Standing on Earth, not rapt above the Pole"(23).

> More safe I Sing with mortal voice, unchang'd
> To hoarce or mute, though fall'n on evil dayes,
> On evil dayes though fall'n, and evil tongues;
> In darkness, and with dangers compast round,
> And solitude.
>
> (VII, 24-28)

The whole book is intended to be melodious and sonorous, the opposite, that is, of hoarse or mute. More important still is the realization that the poetry is song. We are to hear, not merely to visualize, the descriptions. Except for introductory and transitional passages, both Book VII and Book VIII are to be accepted as spoken, not written. We are to attend to the voices of Raphael and Adam as audible discourse. The events of the Creation and the debates about astronomy and Adam's proper attitude toward Eve are to happen to us as sound, not simply as incident and ratiocination.

The point must be dwelt on, for since Milton's day the concept of epic poetry as bardic has declined and a habit of eye-reading has done much to weaken the auditory impact of verse. Comparatively few people seem to be aware that for a very long time after the invention of writing people read not only by moving their lips but also by producing audible sounds. A long digression might be written on the subject, although admittedly not all the facts are clear. We learn from the *Confessions* of St. Augustine that Ambrose astonished him in the fourth century by turning the pages of a book without giving any other sign of reading.[1] Many ancient scripts were not phonetic and may well have required translation into sound; and the earliest Greek script known to us, the Linear B deciphered in the early 1950s by Michael Ventris and John Chadwick, was so imprecise phonetically that one set of symbols could often be read in more than one way. Reading aloud, by providing an auditory context, must often have assisted the choice. Even the later Greek and Latin alphabets were for many centuries written awkwardly—without spaces between the words, with words divided arbitrarily at the ends of lines, in lines running from left to right and then back from right to left (*boustrophedon*). The modern scholar must often try the combinations of letters on his tongue in order to puzzle out a meaning, just as an English-speaking person who has learned the *kana* syllabary used in Japan for foreign terms must often pronounce such a combination as *inishachibu* or *wanmankaa* aloud before he discovers that they are equivalents for "initiative" and "one-man car" (a bus in which the driver also collects the tickets). All this lies so far behind modern Westerners that a sympathetic effort of imagination is necessary to realize how long it must have taken for writing to become an autonomous mode of communication in societies which were mostly illiterate. In recent years, there have even been efforts in the United States to make young people cease having any auditory images at all while reading. The effect on poetry has been bad and has tended to remove us still farther from an understanding of how

[1] *Sed cum legebat, oculi ducebantur per paginas et cor intellectum rimabatur, vox autem et lingua quiescebant* (*Confessionum Libri XIII*, vi, 3). Augustine speculates about possible reasons for this curious practice.

vigorous the notion of poetry as sound remained for Milton.

The insistence that epic poetry is song has begun with the invocation to Book I ("Sing Heav'nly Muse") and has been repeated in each of the succeeding invocations. To labor the point would be useless; whatever his sensory responses to them may have been, even the most eye-minded reader can hardly have failed to notice such phrases as "adventrous *Song*" (I, 13; my italics, as in the remainder of this paragraph and the whole of the next), "With other *notes* then to th' Orphean Lyre/ I *sung* of Chaos and Eternal Night" (III, 17-18), "Smit with the love of sacred *Song*" (III, 29), "thoughts, that voluntarie move/ *Harmonious numbers*; as the wakeful Bird/ *Sings* darkling" (III, 37-39), and now in the passages we have noticed from the invocation to Book VII. The pattern continues beyond the two books with which we are presently concerned—notably in the invocation to Book IX, where Milton remarks gratefully that his Celestial Patroness

> deignes
> Her nightly visitation unimplor'd,
> And dictates to me slumbring, or inspires
> Easie my unpremeditated Verse:
> Since first this Subject for *Heroic Song*
> Pleas'd me.

> (IX, 21-26)

In later books the emphasis is less strong, perhaps because the point has been sufficiently made, perhaps because the tone becomes more conversational after the scenes have been amply set by descriptions and monologues. But there can be no doubt that for Milton the auditory impression throughout is that of a chanting voice. The tradition of chanting is mostly dead now. Perhaps that is one reason why *Paradise Lost* has, until recently, provoked more resistance than, for instance, Donne's less sonorous, less obviously musical, style. The movement has been away from music, as away from grandeur, from "stilts," toward the prosaic and colloquial. To us elevation is suspect because it suggests insincerity, a valuing of something higher than truth. But for Milton epic poetry, as well as lyric, was closely akin to song. As C. S. Lewis has remarked, he is nearer to the Homeric *aoidós*, mounted on a dais and wearing a wreath as he strums his harp, than to the novelist with whom we tend instinctively to identify him.

In Book VII we are again reminded frequently that the visual images are mediated by a voice. "*Say*, Goddess, what ensu'd" (40); "He [Adam] with his consorted Eve/ The storie *heard* attentive" (50-51); "Proceeded thus to *ask* his Heav'nly Guest" (69). All this, and more, in the second paragraph of the book, which contains only thirty lines. The pattern continues. "Great things, and full of wonder *in our eares*,/ . . . thou hast reveald" (70-71); "Deign to descend now lower, and *relate*" (84); "the great Light of Day . . . suspense in Heav'n/ *Held by thy voice, thy potent voice he heares*" (98-100); "thy *audience*" (105); "till thy *Song*/ End" (107-108). This much, again, inside the succeeding forty lines. Milton has done as much as anyone could fairly expect to create in his readers an awareness that the whole substance of this part of his poem is speech which has the quality of song. If we forget that the description is oral, the fault is not his. There are other references to speech and song in lines 72-74, 77-78, 80-81, 94, 109-10, 111, 117-18, 131-32, 138, 174, 192, 221, 230, 243, 252, and 253. At the very end of the book Raphael summarizes:

> thy request think now fulfilld, that *askd*
> How first this World and face of things began,
> And what before thy memorie was don
> From the beginning, that posteritie
> *Informd* by thee might know; if else thou seekst

Aught, not surpassing human measure, *say*.
(VII, 635-40)

"Askd," "informd," "say." The whole book has consisted of speech—that of Adam to Raphael, of Raphael to Adam, of the Father to the Son, of the Son to the chaotic elements whose creation into form He is accomplishing—and of what is explicitly called song, as when we are told that the admiring angels *sung* creation and the six days' acts (601). A visual minded reader is likely to forget the sounds, at least with the conscious part of his mind, as he watches, with absorption, the tremendous ocular images heave themselves into place on a canvas as large as the universe. But that is because, as a modern, he does not really hear poetry. Like prose, poetry has gone a long way toward becoming "mute." In a sense, the auditory imagery of Books VII and VIII—as of all the other books—includes every word.

The song-like quality of the verse of course depends heavily on the rhythms. Milton's blank verse, which is now recognized as a development not of dramatic blank verse but of rhymed heroic verse, treats the individual line as an unusually stable rhythmic unit. The lines end almost regularly in long syllables; and the syntax is so arranged as to permit, more often than in most blank verse, a perceptible if often slight pause at the end of the lines. These characteristics have been obscured by a tendency to insist, in a way truly, that the verse paragraph is Milton's basic compositional unit.

The long syllables I have mentioned are not merely those which contain "long vowels," as those are spoken of in connection with English spelling and pronunciation, but include all the syllables which take a relatively long time to pronounce. Properly, a long vowel is not one with a special quality, like the *a* in "fate" as opposed to the *a* in "bad," but rather one on which the voice dwells for an appreciable instant. An

139

example would be the *a* in "art," which is drawn out as compared to the much shorter *a* in "artistic." Again, the syllable
may be long although the vowel is short. Thus "wing" is
long as compared with "win," or "midst" as compared with
"mid." The length with which we are concerned is of these
two kinds only. The distinction between long and short exists
in most languages but is not distinctly noticed by most
speakers of English. In French each syllable of *été* is short in
spite of the fact that the equivalent English vowel sound, *ay*,
is normally long, whereas the *a* of *âme* is long. In German,
the *a* of *Vater* is long and that of *Wasser* short. In certain
dialects of English—for example, Southern American and
some varieties of Midwestern American—the differences are
less clear; but I take as the norm in what follows standard
British and American dialects in which the distinctions are
regularly if unconsciously observed.

For the sake of unprejudiced examination, let us look at
the terminal sounds of the first five lines in a number of successive verse paragraphs in Book VII.

    1-5: name, [di]vine, soare, wing, thou
  40-44: [*Rapha*]el, [fore]warnd, [be]ware,
      Heav'n² [be]fall
  70-74: eares, [re]veald, sent, [fore]warne, loss
 109-13: [be]sought, milde, askt, works, [suf]fice
 131-35: Heav'n, Host, [a]mong, Deep, [re]turnd

Of these, only "[Rapha]el" in line 40 fails clearly to have
length of the kind described. If only one syllable of twenty-
five violates the norm, the principle of agreeable variation
might be invoked; and perhaps the matter might be left

---

² For Darbishire's "Heaven," which I think is a mistake. The line is
decasyllabic—always important in *Paradise Lost*—without the extra syllable
and contains no opportunities for elision. Columbia has "Heaven" also, and
there seem to be no important textual variants; but we must not forget that
Milton's dictation could easily be misunderstood in detail.

there. Milton's hearing of "Raphael" was perhaps influenced, however, by the Italian "Raffaelo," where the stress comes on "-el" and the vowel is long. Further, Milton sometimes enjoyed giving a syllable uncolloquial weight. He would have been supported in doing so by the sections of Aristotle's *Poetics* (xxi, 2, and xxii, 4-7) which recommend the arbitrary lengthening or shortening of syllables in order to differentiate the language of poetry from that of prose. Those sections now seem unhistorical in their failure to recognize that Homer's verse preserved archaic formulas from a time when Greek was in a preclassical state; but they would have been authoritative for Milton. For the rest, his short terminal syllables can mostly be explained as assuming classical principles of scansion. "[Dispos]sest," in line 142, will illustrate. According to many Renaissance treatises on poetry, a syllable was long if it contained a long vowel or ended with a consonant. For the latter reason, *sub* (if it preceded a consonant) and the first syllable of *circumspicere* would have been counted long; and so with "[dispos]est," in which the final syllable is doubly "closed." Occasionally Milton is misled by the principle, which is dubious, or worse, in its application to English, into believing that a syllable is long or protracted in utterance when it really is not. For the most part, however, his ear was better than his theory, and in general the line-endings are strong.

The further marking of the line terminations by pauses required—or allowed—by the syntax is more exceptionable but still important. The following passage, chosen at random from the middle of a book (where Milton is neither introducing a fresh subject nor concluding one but is in full career) is fairly typical.

God saw,
Surveying his great Work, that it was good:

For of Celestial Bodies first the Sun
A mightie Spheare he fram'd, unlightsom first,
Though of Ethereal Mould: then formd the Moon
Globose, and everie magnitude of Starrs,
And sowd with Starrs the Heav'n thick as a field:
Of Light by farr the greater part he took,
Transplanted from her cloudie Shrine, and plac'd
In the Suns Orb, made porous to receive
And drink the liquid Light, firm to retaine
Her gatherd beams, great Palace now of Light.

(VII, 352-63)

The proportion of run-on lines in this excerpt is roughly normal. Since I intend in later parts of the chapter to speak frequently of enjambment, I do not wish to deny that Milton's rhythms frequently carry across the line-ends. Nevertheless enjambment has many degrees, and in *Paradise Lost* the carrying on of the sense usually does not prevent a slight terminal pause. Indeed, a pause often assists the understanding of meaning by suggesting groupings other than those into which the voice might otherwise fall.

What is meant by the last statement can best be shown by analysis. In the third and fourth lines of the passage, "A mightie Spheare" might be thought to stand in apposition with "Sun," thus: "He framed the sun ↘/ a mighty sphere ↘/ unlightsome first . . ." If, however, we agree with Miss Darbishire that Milton was careful about his punctuation, the lack of pointing around the appositive element becomes significant. Let us read straight on across the line-end *except* for a slight upward inflection on "Sun" and a tiny pause after it: "the Sun ↗/ A mightie Spheare he fram'd. . . ." We now perceive that the sun was framed *as* a mighty sphere. Technically, "A mightie Spheare" is a retained object. The difference is identical with that between "Roger, the captain of the team" (apposition) and "We elected Roger captain" (retained object). And this reading is not only different but better, for it makes the act of framing more positive, gives it more vigor.

So with most of the other enjambments. "Globose," in the sixth line, is not a displaced adjective modifying "Moon" but another retained object: "then formd the Moon ↗/ *Globose*." The word tells how the moon was formed and does not merely remind us of its rotund shape. Thereafter the lines are end-stopped until, near the end, we arrive at three successive enjambments across "plac'd," "receive," and "retaine." A brief pause on "plac'd," again with a slight upward turn of the voice, by putting extra value on the verb makes it a shade more active. In order not to press too hard, I shall not attempt to make similar arguments about "receive" and "retaine" but will urge merely that the preservation of the regular rhythmic pattern, though perhaps with a little weakening here, will produce a more pleasing effect, and one probably nearer to what Milton intended, than a careless ignoring of the decasyllabic pattern. Occasional obscuring of the pattern—as opposed to destruction of it—gives the verse vitality by causing it to play against natural speech tendencies. But we ought not to forget that the lines are poetry. They should never be read with the rhythmic freedom of prose. The approximation to chant must be maintained consistently.

There will be resistance to this advice, for nowadays we approve freedom and dislike the submitting of expression to predetermined limits. Milton's contemporaries had different attitudes, as may be suggested by a cross-cultural comparison— again with Japan, where material progress coexists with a good deal of aesthetic traditionalism. In *Noh*, in *kabuki*, in *bunraku* (a puppet drama in which very large puppets are manipulated by "invisible" operators wearing black), and in *kōwaka-mai*, a sort of quasi-epic accompanied by music and

143

dancing but not by imitative gesture, everything possible is done to "distance" the performance from contemporary reality in order to give it dignity. The actors or singers recite in extraordinary, rather "strangled," voices, they separate syllables much more distinctly than in colloquial speech, the diction and syntax are decidedly archaic, the rhythms tend strongly toward chant, and there is a musical accompaniment on *samisen* or drums, or both. And these artificialities, far from exasperating, obviously delight the audiences. Something of the same artificiality was characteristic of "primary" epic generally. We know that the Homeric and Germanic bards struck rhythmically on a harp or harp-like instrument. Although Milton lived in the modern period, his conception of poetry was traditional. Also, he lived before the novel, by moving as far as possible toward realism, had assisted the destruction of formality. Equalitarian social theories had not as yet made men suspicious of ceremony. Different as modern conceptions of poetry are, it is still possible for intellectually flexible readers to meet him more or less on his own terms; and doing so, I suggest, carries a considerable reward.[3]

If what has been said is correct, Milton's auditory awareness shows itself everywhere in Books VII and VIII merely in the rhythmic qualities of the verse. We must now descend to details; but before we do so I should like to offer a rather elaborate explanation of the methods which will be used. Certain common assumptions about poetic sound will be denied and certain unusual discriminations made.

It will be best to work with a sample passage.

> Joyous the Birds; fresh Gales[4] and gentle Aires

[3] The argument just concluded arose partly as a result of exposure to Oriental performing arts but also partly as the result of a whole day spent in hearing *Paradise Lost* read by members of a Milton seminar. By far the most impressive part of the reading was the most strongly rhythmic; and the whole class agreed that this was the way Milton "ought to be read."

[4] Mr. Kakuaki Saito, of International Christian University, Tokyo, has sug-

Whisperd it to the Woods, and from thir wings
Flung Rose, flung Odours from the spicie Shrub,
Disporting, till the amorous Bird of Night
Sung Spousal, and bid haste the Eevning Starr
On his Hill top, to light the bridal Lamp.

(VIII, 515-20)

I choose the above from Book VIII, which because of limitations of space will be slighted in the remainder of the chapter. The verse here *sounds right*. Observe, we might say, the
cheerful resonance of the vowels in "Joyous the Birds"; note
the coolness of the phrase "fresh Gales" and the drop to softness in "gentle Aires"; see how skillfully the poet has suggested whispering by filling the second line with *w*'s, and
how in the third and fourth lines the rich concentration of
o-sounds implies the energy with which the puffs of wind
disseminate fragrance and, a moment later, the nightingale
begins its song. All this may seem fairly plausible. At any
rate it is no more wild than many discussions of poetic sound.
Yet I fear that it is mostly sheer fancy.

One trouble is the usual one of confusing spellings with
sounds. The *o*'s in lines three and four ought not, any modern
linguist will say impatiently, to be considered together because they stand for quite different vowels. The *o* of "Rose"
and the first *o* of "Odours" are "close" (pronounced *oh*); the
first *o* of "amorous" and that in the *ou* combination of the
last syllable are *schwa* (the slurred sound of the *a* in "comma"); that of "disporting" is "open" (pronounced *aw*). The
chance that they are all symbolized by squiggles containing
an *o* is acoustically quite irrelevant. Again, "Whisperd" does

---

gested to me that "Gales" suggests nightingales. I find the suggestion interesting: Milton may have been thinking about nightingales when he needed
a word for "wind." But I do not believe that he had read Empson or consciously sought to be cleverly indirect—as the inappropriateness of "fresh" to
nightingales indicates.

not begin with a *w*-sound but with an *h*-sound, since the digraph *wh* is pronounced, where it is differentiated from a simple *w* (as presumably it still was for Milton), as though the letters were reversed.[5] Most critical discussions of poetic sound are filled with similar misstatements. It is one of the reasons why persons who have a little more than the usual understanding of phonetics are impatient about nearly everything that is written concerning the sound values of poetry.

We may, however, go further. I propose to dwell briefly on the phrases "fresh Gales" and "gentle Aires," which to my ear do indeed seem to be, respectively, rather fresh and rather gentle. The best test of the impression is to make what I call phonemic anagrams. A phonemic anagram differs from the usual anagram in disregarding spellings to focus on actual sounds. For example, "ether" is a spelling anagram of "three" because it contains the same five letters; but it is not a phonemic anagram because it has an extra syllable. "Three" is a monosyllable, "ether" a dissyllable; the initial *e* of "ether" is identical in sound with the *ee* of "three," so that the extra *e* of the latter has been freed to make a separate syllable with *r*. In contrast, "tile" is an accurate phonemic anagram of "light" because the three sounds, *t, eye,* and *l,* have been rearranged in a different order.

If we scramble all the sounds of the two phrases "fresh Gales" and "gentle Aires" we may come out, although not with absolute exactness, with the two acceptable equivalents "grave shells" and "lent chairs." The only differences are that in the first an *f* has been replaced by a *v* and in the second a soft *g* by a *ch*. Since a *v* is voiced, whereas an *f* is not, the change should actually increase the resonance of the first phrase; and no reason appears why the second change should alter the total effect drastically. If the constituent sounds *qua* sounds suggest freshness and gentleness, the phonemic ara-

___

[5] *Hw* was the Anglo-Saxon spelling, as in *hwæt* for modern "what."

grams ought to do so also; but they clearly do not. We may now take a further step in order to see whether an analysis of the two phrases together may restore acoustic values not present in them separately. Scrambling *all* the phonemes in "fresh Gales and gentle Aires," we may arrive at a grotesque utterance which appears to urge upon a rather oddly mixed audience an action symbolizing the destruction of hopes: "Girl, gent, friends—lay ashes!" The phonemes here are exactly identical with those of "fresh Gales and gentle Aires" except that the *eh* sound of "gentle" has been lowered to the slurred second vowel of "ashes." Or, again, even more outrageously: "Ashes! Gent, lay friend's girl!" The phonemes are the same as before.[6] But neither transformation gives anything like the acoustic impression we thought we had derived from the original. We may therefore decide fairly confidently that the acoustic effectiveness of the half-line cannot be the result of Milton's having chosen precisely these individual phonemes instead of other possible ones.

By making a different approach we may achieve a better result; but the reader should be warned in advance that he will probably sense strain in some of the following comments. The reasons, I think, are mainly two. First, in reading a poetic excerpt for the purpose of noting auditory qualities one inevitably reads more slowly and attentively than ordinarily. As has been said, modern reading habits have been formed on prose, and many persons read chiefly with their eyes. Training in declamation (what in the last century was called "elocution" in American schools) is rare today. Even teachers of literature read, probably, a great deal more prose than poetry (including newspapers, current magazines, academic treatises, and novels), and much of the time

[6] My transcription of the Miltonic phrase is the following: "freʃ geɪlz ænd dʒentəl ɛ·rz." In the anagrams, "girl" is read as "gɔrl." Of course some acoustic phenomena are disregarded—e.g., the length of the vowel in "Aires."

they are trying to get on as fast as possible. The effort to interpret sound values makes essential not only slow reading but also repeated oral experimentation; and this may lead gradually to the perception of acoustic hints that remain opaque to readers who refuse to try the phrases again and again on their tongues. Secondly, explanations must often be overstated because the linguistic forms available for the communication of acoustic phenomena are very gross. We do not, indeed, even have a commonly known phonetic alphabet, so that I have had to invent such symbols as *eh* for the *e* in "gentle" and *eye* for the *i* in "tile." What exists in the ear as the tiniest possible stimulus to response must often be described as if it were stronger than it really is.

If we now return to the passage quoted above, the fitnesses of sounds to meanings seem less noteworthy than before. Nevertheless something may perhaps be salvaged. "Joyous the Birds" may sound slightly energetic because the stressing of the first syllable instead of the usual second implies, by a sort of acoustic metaphor, an eagerness which does not allow the poet to wait for the second syllable to emphasize something. The same inversion occurs elsewhere, but here the meaning of the words affects, or may affect, our response to the sound. We hear "DA di di DA" instead of "di DA di DA," and the fact that the words proclaim joyousness suggests that joy is the motive of the alteration. Also, the *oy* sound of "joyous" is a "rising" diphthong because the sound moves upward in the resonance chamber of the mouth from the fairly deep position of *aw* to the higher one of short *i*; but this may happen too quickly to be significant. In the second line, "Whisperd it to the Woods, and from thir wings," the *hw* of "Whisperd" is in fact a "breathy" sound which can be taught to nonnative speakers by requiring them to breathe strongly upon their hands. The effect is not so much a whisper, the action the word names, as a puff; and the subject here is precisely "Gales" and "Aires." Although "Woods" and "wings" do not exactly alliterate with "Whisperd," they pick up one-half of the compound initial consonant and, by repeating it twice within the same line, prolong somewhat our sense of its value. In the next line, the phrase "Flung Rose, flung Odours . . ." suggests distantly the quick movements of flinging, as of a sower scattering seed; but the hint is the barest possible, since the second phrase runs on through four more words. The technique is appropriate to a good narrator who implies the physical movements of his characters by gestures so quick and incomplete that they may escape conscious notice. The actor works differently because instead of hinting he must perform. If a stage direction reads, "He springs to his feet," the actor must do so. When a narrator recites the words, he may, in contrast, satisfy himself with the merest flick of his hand or the smallest possible raising of his shoulders. As epic and not drama, *Paradise Lost* requires not the performance but only the gesture. Moving on, we come to "the amorous Bird of Night/ Sung Spousal . . ." Since the nightingale is one of the birds whose energy we have been made to appreciate, we may feel subconsciously the appropriateness of the enjambment. The verse flows across the line-end as the song is characterized by its flow. For the rest, so far as I can see, the beauty of the passage results from poetic data other than acoustic. And some of the acoustic adjustments I have noticed are, I confess, on the borderline between the demonstrable and the probably imaginary. Nevertheless I believe that results can best be sought in such directions as these comments indicate rather than in the more usual discussions of affective values supposed to attach to isolated phonemes and syllables.

Returning to Book VII we may look first at the creative speeches of the Son, himself the Word, who by speaking words frames Earth, the heaven of stars and planets, and the life by which Earth is to be vitalized.

> And thou my Word, begott'n Son, by thee
> This I perform, speak thou, and be it don.
> (VII, 163-64)

Surely here, if anywhere, the sound will be rich, evocative, *creative*. If auditory qualities are to resemble meanings, we may expect them to do so in speeches which call into being the objects that are named. God's speech is presumably perfect speech; and in Milton's day the belief was by no means dead, though it may have sunk partly out of consciousness, that the name in some degree is the thing. Behind Adam's naming of the creatures in *Genesis* lies a primitive assumption still current in undeveloped cultures that knowledge of the name confers power over the object.

The expectation is disappointed. The creative speeches are as little onomatopoeic as any in the entire poem.

> Let ther be Light, said God . . .
> (VII, 243)

> let ther be Firmament
> Amid the Waters, and let it divide
> The Waters from the Waters . . .
> (VII, 261-63)

> Be gatherd now ye Waters under Heav'n
> Into one place, and let dry Land appeer.
> (VII, 283-84)

So with the rest. Aside from a certain authority in the intonations there is no special adaptation; and the reason is at once apparent. Milton is following as exactly as possible the wording in *Genesis*, not poeticizing to the top of his bent. His respect for Holy Writ overrides at this point his commitment to his art. He knows confidently the places at which his readers will expect literal fidelity to the Biblical record. He can invent speeches, but he cannot contradict what God has actually said. His best course will be simply to make rhythm out of the English equivalent of the more authentic Hebrew; and this comes easily enough except in line 262, where the standard alternation of stressed and unstressed syllables would force us to read "aMID the WAters, AND let IT diVIDE." But this is near enough if the reading is half-chanted and not held too strictly to prose accentuation, which would shift the stresses and telescope the normal five feet into four or three. The example helps to justify, retrospectively, what has been said about the proper mode of recitation. In Book X Milton will again be forced to adopt Old Testament wording when the Son judges the Parents and the serpent; and there—since the judgment is crucial to the whole poem—the metrical form will be strained to the limit and perhaps beyond.

Elsewhere better opportunities arise for representing the meaning in the sound. In Book VII, I take it, Milton's main concern is visual, not auditory. In his mind's eye he pictures the greater part of chaos being excluded by the turning of the golden compasses in space and then watches, rather than hears, the area within the sphere achieving order at the divine words which he cannot report otherwise than as in Scripture. Nevertheless he is a poet, and he appreciates the fitness of expression to idea; so the flow of sound from the cooperating reader's lips frequently imitates, in one way or another, the actions or attitudes which are being described.

The simplest procedure will be to observe a few representative passages in the order in which they occur.

> still govern thou my Song,
> *Urania*, and fit audience find, though few:

But drive farr off the barbarous dissonance
Of *Bacchus* and his Revellers, the Race
Of that wilde Rout that tore the *Thracian* Bard
In *Rhodope*, where Woods and Rocks had Eares
To rapture, till the savage clamor dround
Both Harp and Voice; nor could the Muse defend
Her Son.

(VII, 30-38)

After the introductory line and a half the note deepens: "Drive
farr off the barbarous dissonance . . ." There is no dissonance;
creating harsh verse would be a cheap victory. Except for
the loose *schwa* sounds and the middle high *i* of "dissonance,"
however, the vowels are all protracted back-vowels;[7] and the
trilled intervocallic *r*'s (in Milton's pronunciation) of "farr
off" and "-barous" add further resonance. The *r*'s of "farr"
and "barbarous" are picked up by the *r*'s (also trilled?) of
"Revellers," "Race," "Rout," "Rhodope," "Rocks," and "rapture," as they had been anticipated by the trilled *r* of "Urania,"
so that there is hardness, if not harshness, in the passage
(Milton pronounced the letter *r* "very hard" and with
satirical effect); and this is appropriate to disapproval of
revelry and violence. At the end the tone descends to regretful
quietness: "nor could the Muse defend/ Her Son." The verse
has risen to clamorousness as it described clamor, but when
enough has been said it sinks to patient acceptance. (The emotional pattern is characteristic of Milton's response to frustration, from *Sonnet VII* to *Paradise Regained*.) Like any
auditory effects, the modifications can be obscured by a wooden
reading. The passage itself, however, not only motivates but
gently insists on a crescendo followed by a depressed but un-
complaining diminuendo.

A quite different effect is sought a little further on.

---

[7] Except that the *i* of "drive," which begins as an *ah*, rises to short *i* (as
in "did").

> as one whose drouth
> Yet scarce allayd still eyes the current streame,
> Whose liquid murmur heard new thirst excites,
> Proceeded thus to ask his Heav'nly Guest.
>
> (VII, 66-69)

Here again the poet avoids bravura techniques. The running ("current") stream runs for a single line, and within that chiefly through three words, "liquid murmur heard." Keats or Tennyson would have done more. It is one sign of their lesser stature, their tendency to poetic excess. Milton's line is softer even than the occasion would permit, for "current" suggests a more lively movement than is implied by the four-times repeated—and thrice protracted—*ur* sound of "murmur," "heard," and "thirst." The running of the stream is evidently gentle, though strong enough to produce a liquid sound attractive to a man whose thirst has been partly slaked.

Acoustic imagery is not limited to the verbal imitation of actual noises. In the following excerpt the word "suspense" is pointed by a vocal rise terminated by a pause at a relatively high pitch, so that the auditory pattern becomes a metaphor of the meaning.

> And the great Light of Day yet wants to run
> Much of his Race though steep, suspense in Heav'n
> Held by thy voice, thy potent voice he heares,
> And longer will delay to heare thee tell
> His Generation, and the rising Birth
> Of Nature from the unapparent Deep.
>
> (VII, 98-103)

The usual drop of the voice at a comma is partly compromised in line two by the fact that the vowel of "steep" is the "highest" vowel in English and occurs in a word which itself suggests height. If a pause is inserted here, and another rather sharp

153

and dramatic one after "Heav'n," with a slow descent through "Held by thy voice" and the resumption of normal speed and fuller resonance in "thy potent voice he heares," the curve of the sound will approximate that of the thought.

In lines which follow immediately, a pause is again important, but this time it is combined with an exceptionally strong enjambment through "bring" to produce silence at a place where silence is mentioned.

> Or if the Starr of Eevning and the Moon
> Haste to thy audience, Night with her will bring
> Silence, and Sleep listning to thee will watch.
>
> (VII, 104-106)

A little further on, Raphael keeps Lucifer in Heaven briefly before his fall by a parenthesis from which he slopes rapidly into Hell.

> after *Lucifer* from Heav'n
> (So call him, brighter once amidst the Host
> Of Angels, then that Starr the Starrs among)
> Fell with his flaming Legions . . .
>
> (VII, 131-34)

A pointing finger locates the archangel in his forfeited eminence and then follows his descent, which is implicitly—and quite appropriately, since Lucifer is a name for the planet Venus—compared to that of a falling star. Although the imagery here is not merely auditory, the suspension of Lucifer in the sky is achieved partly by a syntactical structure which guides the voice.

Other manipulations of vocal patterns occur elsewhere. After the announcement of God's creative purpose the difference between speech and song is marked by a change of accentuation.

> Great triumph and rejoycing was in Heav'n

When such was heard declar'd th' Almightie's will;
Glorie they sung to the most High, good will
To future men . . .

(VII, 180-83)

"GLORie they SUNG to the MOST HIGH, GOOD WILL"
—not the usual alternation of unstressed and stressed, but a
reversal in the first foot, a pyrrhic in the third, and then two
spondees. The effect is metrically disruptive, as it should be to
signalize a shift from poetic chant to outright hymning. The
interpretation is not compromised by the fact that the line is
partly quoted from *Luke*. The poet can find values in his
donnée, as a sculptor can take hints from the grain in wood.

All the effects so far noticed are subtle. It is not Milton's
practice, in his mature poems, to write flashily, to set down
"Crash!" and "Bang!" and "Boom!" to indicate clatter, to
invent a lyrical verse pattern to describe a brook bickering
down a valley, to fill his lines with *o*'s to render the golden
tones of bells. Because his poetic sensitivity is greater, his ear
needs less stimulus; so his method is both simpler and harder.
Coleridge's description of a nightingale ("precipitates/ With
fast thick warble his delicious notes," "The Nightingale,"
44-45) is nearer to Milton's way than is Keats' or Shelley's.
Moreover, besides needing less stimulus himself, Milton
trusts his fit audience to need less. For example, the sudden
alteration of meter just noticed is dropped after a single line.
Thereafter the elevation persists while the meter, except for
one inversion in the second line, reasserts the epic norm:

To future men, and in thir dwellings peace:
Glorie to him whose just avenging ire
Had driven out th' ungodly from his sight . . .

(VII, 183-85)

The repetition of "Glorie" in the first foot of the second line

155

prevents the transition from being too abrupt and thus briefly prolongs the onomatopoeic gesture. But it it only a gesture. Except in Books I and II, where Milton was perhaps still experimenting, his practice is to offer no more. As time passed, the habit of giving only the barest hints of the proper response grew upon him, until in *Paradise Regained*, which is in his maturest style, the demands on the reader's perceptivity, to judge from the response even of many "good" readers, became excessive.

It is true, then, that the acoustic modulations in Books VII and VIII are unobtrusive. What used to be called Milton's magnificent roll of sound obscures the constant delicate adjustments made in accordance with local demands. Yet the adjustments are there and become increasingly apparent as familiarity with the epic grows. Everybody can perceive the auditory fitness of the underlined phrase in the following passage:

> Heav'n op'nd wide
> Her ever during Gates, *Harmonious sound*
> *On gold'n Hinges moving*, to let forth
> The King of Glorie, in his powerful Word
> And Spirit coming to create new Worlds.
>
> (VII, 205-209)

But the round openness of "op'nd" and the temporal width of "wide" are less obvious, and the superior weight of "powerful Word" over the comparatively light "Spirit," which is suitable because of the greater importance of words in the creative process ("speak thou, and be it don"—VII, 164), may be noticed only when attention is focused specifically on sound. When the disorder of Chaos is mentioned the verse is capable of imitating that too, with the same lack of emphasis:

> They viewd the vast immeasurable Abyss

Outrageous as a Sea, dark, wasteful, wilde,
Up from the bottom turnd by furious windes
And surging waves . . .

(VII, 211-14)

The three caesuras in the second line impede the smooth flow
of the verse, whereas the strong gusts mentioned in the third
blow right through the line and even carry on into the
fourth. The effects, however, are again subdued.

So it is often. The imposition of peace on the warring elements is wonderfully simple in its effect in spite of the concealed sophistication of the poetic means.

Silence, ye troubl'd waves, and thou Deep, peace,
Said then th' Omnific Word, your discord end.

(VII, 216-17)

A pause after "Silence" to suit the sound to the command, a
momentary stillness of the speaking voice (though not, of
course, of the poetry) after "peace" across the angel's quiet
interpellation to the final brief and authoritative "your discord
end," with which the sentence also ends: all this gives the
impression not only of ease but also of perfect confidence.
No more than eleven words are spoken, and these are divided
into five phrases, all uttered with the downward inflection
of a general ending war games. Such fitness as these do not
challenge notice but reward it when freely given.

Even the basically visual Book VII contains too much that
is auditorily noteworthy to permit more than a few random
samplings such as these. The quasi-exhaustiveness attempted
at some points in the present study is out of the question here.
All the transitions from speech to song repay examination;
I choose one additional example to serve for the rest.

with joy and shout
The hollow Universal Orb they filld,

And touchd thir Gold'n Harps, and hymning prais'd
God and his works, Creatour him they sung.
(VII, 256-59)

The long vowel-sounds of "joy," "shout," "Orb," "Gold'n,"
"Harps," and "prais'd," the syllables made long by consonant
clusters in "filld," "touchd," and "hymning," and the doubling
of the effect in "Gold'n" and "prais'd," where syllables containing vowels long by nature are made longer by terminal
consonants, again deepen the resonance to song; and the last
phrase, which itself achieves weight if the nasals in "him"
and "sung" are a little protracted, also suggests formality by
the rhetorical inversion of normal order. This time, however,
the iambic stress is modified only by an inversion in the
fourth line, and a change of movement is attained chiefly by
a special oratundity which half suppresses the normal line-end
pause after "shout" and "prais'd." Similar felicities can be
found almost everywhere, no matter what the immediate subject. Only it must be insisted that the modifications are slight,
that they are meant to register on an acute ear and not to call
blatantly for admiration. Milton does not write program
music but rather aims at a persistent musicality.

A few additional comments only can be afforded, the
passages being chosen not for their brilliance but for their
typicality. The gathering of the waters into one place is
described as follows:

So high as heav'd the tumid Hills, so low
Down sunk a hollow bottom broad and deep,
Capacious bed of Waters: thither they
Hasted with glad precipitance, uprowld
As drops on dust conglobing from the drie . . .
(VII, 288-92)

The diphthongal *i* of "high," which begins as an *ah* and

rises to a short *i* (as in *did*), is succeeded by the still higher *ee* sound of "heav'd," then drops to *i-oo* in "tumid," only to rise again to the *i* of "Hills." The vowels of "so low" slide back a little further in the mouth, and the resonance next ascends very slightly to the initial *ah* of the diphthong in "Down" only to sink deeper still in the *ŏŏ* which finishes the sound and to reach, finally, the nadir of English vowels in the *uh* of "sunk." In general, the sound curves upward to imitate the thrust of the hills and then drops with the water. In "Hasted with glad precipitance," after the first long vowel come seven short syllables which accelerate the movement; and the length of "conglobing" demonstrates faintly the swelling of the crisper "drops on dust." Here, too, however, the rise is not to a shriek, and the drop is not to a rumble. A slight variation will accomplish as much as is needed.

At times, of course, the artistry descends to outright onomatopoeia, but seldom for long, and seldom strikingly. No better —or more unexpected—word than "clang" could have been used to describe the sound of a covey of birds rising suddenly from the ground:[8]

> summ'd thir Penns, and soaring th' air sublime
> With clang despis'd the ground.
>
> (VII, 421-22)

Coleridge's description of a nightingale's song has been cited; Milton's has less speed and more softness and also calls less insistently for notice:

> nor then the solemn Nightingal
> Ceas'd warbling, but all night tun'd her soft layes. . . .
>
> (VII, 435-36)

The slowing of the second line is achieved by a weighting with

---

[8] "Clang" seems, however, to have been a semi-technical term for the "shrill scream of birds" (*NED*).

long vowels and a multiplication of stresses: "CEAS'D
WARBling, but ALL NIGHT TUN'D her SOFT LAYES."
Its softness results from the choice, after the initial *ee*, of the
deep vowels, *aw*, *uh*, *aw*, *eye*, *yoo*, and *aw*. The resonance,
however, having sunk from *ee*, rises again on the final *ay*,
since the sentence does not come to a full stop.

We pass on, reluctantly, to Book VIII, which must be
treated even more summarily than Book VII. The transition
is made as follows:

> The Angel ended, and in *Adams* Eare
> So Charming left his voice, that he a while
> Thought him still speaking, still stood fixt to hear;
> Then as new wak't thus gratefully repli'd.
>
> (VIII, 1-4)

The ending of the angel's speech is marked by the end of a
phrase. The voice is "left" in Adam's ear by another comma,
after which the charmed listener is held expectant for the duration of a phrase which carries smoothly across a line-break. A
terminal pause here would cut in the middle an almost be-
witched anticipation which must be kept rhythmically, as well as
semantically, unitary. The fixing of Adam's posture is assisted
by an emphatic stop at "hear" (which rhymes with "Eare") and
also—less certainly—by the *-kst* ending of "fixt," which is
followed at once by the initial *t* of "to." If the *t* of "fixt" is
completed instead of being left half-finished, like the usual
first consonant of an identical pair (for instance, the *kk* of
"bookcase"), a slight catch prepares for the strong pause at
the semicolon. In the last line the absence of punctuation
implies an unbroken flow which suggests the recovery of
waking energy. Upon this pattern, further, is mounted a
series of vertical changes in pitch. The *-ed* of "ended" slopes
down toward silence, "Eare" begins a rise toward the still
higher pitch of "CHARMing" (which despite its deeper

vowel receives more emphasis than any other word in the passage), and so on. Changes in pitch, however, differ so widely from reading to reading that almost any comments about them will be disputed. And this is unfortunate, since pitch is at least as important to the total sound pattern as phenomena which fluctuate less.[9]

Variations of pitch may be illustrated further by a somewhat later passage.

> Whether the Sun predominant in Heav'n
> Rise on the Earth, or Earth rise on the Sun,
> Hee from the East his flaming rode begin,
> Or Shee from West her silent course advance
> With inoffensive pace that spinning sleeps
> On her soft Axle, while she paces Eev'n,
> And bears thee soft with the smooth Air along,
> Sollicit not thy thoughts with matters hid . . .
>
> (VIII, 160-67)

Whatever auditory adaptation of sound to sense there may be in the first two lines depends primarily on pitch, as that is determined by emphasis. A prose reading would probably come out something like this:

```
                                          Rise
             Sun
                       dom        Heav'n           Earth,
   "Wheth
           er the    pre      inant in        on the

       Earth
     or      rise          Sun"
           on  the
```

[9] The usual tendency seems to be to discuss pitch in terms of "high" and "low" vowels. But "high" and "low" refer to positions in the oral cavity and need not determine pitch—as is shown by the fact that the deep vowel *oo*

The differences are of course only approximate, and anybody could suggest modifications. Nevertheless it is probable that a "sensitive" reading would elevate the first "Rise" a little above the other words, partly because of a hint contained in the meaning, but also partly because the term introduces a new idea and stands, semantically, on a level separate from that of "Sun," "Heav'n," and "Earth," all of which denote astronomical bodies. The second "rise," in contrast, repeats an idea already once introduced and hence requires less emphasis. "Sun" would appear to have the next highest pitch; and this again is appropriate because the sun is "predominant" in the sky.

Other adaptive techniques in the passage have to do chiefly with sound qualities. "Inoffensive pace that spinning sleeps" produces a slight buzz because of the five *s*-sounds—all authentically *s*-sounds, not, as so often in undergraduate analyses, the related ones of *z* or *sh*. Also, the four *n*-sounds, the last a part of the still more strongly nasalized *-ng* combination, result in a faint hum like that made by a top or a smoothly whirring dynamo. The effect is reinforced by the two uses of "soft" and the one of "smooth" in the following two lines, although here the onomatopoeia is partly imaginary. We entertain the meanings and imagine (at least in "soft"; it may be authentically present in "smooth") an auditory approximation. The enjambments also have a part in the total effect. The rising of the sun described in the first two lines ought not to hesitate across a line-end; neither should the "advance" of line four or the spinning pace of line five. Taken as a whole, the passage is fitted to the meaning by both pitch

---

may be sung two octaves higher than the high vowel *ee*. If it were not so, the melodies written for lyrics would be determined almost mechanically by the alternation of vowel sounds. And what of the consonants? *K* is formed farther back in the mouth than *ch*: must "cheek" therefore be sung on three pitches, one for the vowel and different ones for each of the two consonants?

and sound, though delicately and by the least insistent of techniques.

An effect of a quite different kind is produced in Adam's description of his first spoken words.

> to speak I tri'd, and forthwith spake,
> My Tongue obeyd and readily could name
> What e're I saw. Thou Sun, said I, faire Light,
> And thou enlight'nd Earth, so fresh and gay,
> Ye Hills and Dales, ye Rivers, Woods, and Plaines,
> And yee that live and move, fair Creatures, tell,
> Tell, if ye saw, how came I thus, how here?
>
> (VIII, 271-77)

"Readily could name...." Yes, as the cascade of nouns shows: Sun, Light, Earth, Hills, Dales, Rivers, Woods, Plaines, Creatures, all appropriately capitalized. But nouns come more easily than syntax, as in a child's speech, so that the sentence is jerky, proceeds by short bursts. There are pauses, as Adam reports the speech, after two words, after two more, after four, four, four, two, one, two, six, two, one, one, three, four, and two. Accordingly the number of caesuras is unusually large. The speaker is experimenting, and the verse halts with his tongue. He can move only painfully from enumeration to predication; and when he does so, the sentence turns out to be a question which is slowed by four pauses between the first "tell" and the complete stop at the interrogation point. In preparation, the line and a half before the first words run smoothly on to the period. The reporting Adam has achieved a fluency he did not have in his first moments of consciousness.

Another example (we are skipping very rapidly now) appears in Adam's praise of Eve.

> what she wills to do or say,

Seems wisest, vertuousest, discreetest, best;
All higher knowledge in her presence falls
Degraded, Wisdom in discourse with her
Looses discount'nanc't, and like folly shewes. . . .
Greatness of mind and nobleness thir seat
Build in her loveliest, and create an awe
About her, as a guard Angelic plac't.

(VIII, 549-53, 557-59)

"Wisest," "vertuousest," "discreetest," "best," with their separate falling inflections, have the ring of quiet conviction. Is it fanciful to perceive also a special appropriateness in the stressed vowels? Wisdom, we say, is an especially deep form of knowledge, and the diphthongal vowel of "wise" starts far back in the oral cavity and then moves forward, like a mind going out to meet the data of experience. To me, perhaps quite arbitrarily, "vertuousest" sounds *clean*, especially if the last two syllables are given full syllabic value. The Lady in *Comus* might have spoken the word in a clear, fastidious young soprano. "Discreetest," finally, seems thin, as if it implied the delicately scrupulous following of a slender path. "All higher knowledge" we may regard with somewhat greater confidence as relatively high in pitch, partly because the meaning suggests elevation; and "falls" drops easily downward both because of the low vowel and because the voice instinctively follows the described action. The fall continues across the line-end to stop, as if it had hit bottom, at the comma which follows "Degraded." The enjambments in the third and second line from the bottom also have value, the earlier because greatness and nobleness may be felt as resistant to the limits of decasyllabic verse and the latter because the hush of "awe" must be prolonged beyond the usual rhythmic break.

In such ways as these Milton shows keen auditory awareness in two books of *Paradise Lost* which focus, respectively, not upon sound but upon visual imagery and discursive thought. The awareness is partly of sounds as sounds: the poet responds to the acoustic qualities of his own words in an attempt to fit them to the noises made by described objects or to the pattern of "proper" epic verse as that exists in his mind's ear. More often, however, the fitnesses are of a less easily cognized sort, for they have the character rather of acoustic metaphor than of simple mellifluence or onomatopoeic imitation. An attempt has been made to offer examples; and others can be found in profusion. A characteristic of nearly all the fitnesses is subtlety, delicacy, restraint. The poet does not himself require strong stimulus, and he respects his audience sufficiently not to assume that its sensitivity is inferior to his own. In consequence, many of the effects can be appreciated only by an ear which has ceased to be overwhelmed by the resonance of Milton's epic style. The neophyte is likely to be stunned and therefore, for a while, to be incapable of perceiving variations in an orchestral grandeur almost too clamorous to be endured. In time, however, the ear becomes attuned to the roar, and then the delicacies begin to emerge. In the end, astonishment at the subtleties replaces admiration of the crashing bass chords. The combination of such power with such sensitiveness is unusual in English poetry and perhaps in all poetry. It is thus the range of Milton's verse which, in the final analysis, is most impressive. Seldom or nowhere else is such strength of line and mass so beautifully responsive to the requirements of local context.

The workmanship I have attempted to demonstrate is not, of course, the result merely of conscious thought. It can have had no other source than an approximation of total awareness in which cognition far outran what could have been clearly understood by the analytic intelligence. In hearing, as in seeing, Milton was thoroughly awake, keenly attentive, vigorously energized: consistently poised for the sensing, as well as the thinking, of what was happening inside his epic. His own Aristotelian aesthetic could not have been wholly responsible for his achievement, for he worked, as the greatest artists have always worked, with parts of the psyche which have only recently begun to be understood.

....

CHAPTER VIII

SOMATIC

PERCEPTION

Consciousness, as we all know from experience, includes not only thought and perceptions of the external world but much more. Things seem to happen within the body, or *soma*, which we attempt to describe by such phrases as "My heart swelled," "I could hardly sit still," "I was just sick when I heard the news," "I never felt so jittery," and "I was walking on air." The reason, of course, is that the body is in fact involved in states of consciousness. Such physical processes as glandular action, modifications of the circulatory system, and changes in the nerves and muscles accompany, and in part produce, mental phenomena. Some of the processes are comparatively well understood: for example, the pouring of adrenalin into the blood. Others, like changes in respiration, in the pulse rate, in blood pressure, and in neural impulses on the cortex, can be measured or diagramed. A few attract our notice directly—the pounding of the heart which results from sudden fear, a tingling of the scalp sometimes associated with awe. No adequate vocabulary exists for the description of such states. Yet from the beginning poets have recognized and registered, crudely or with skill, a somatic element in consciousness. To the handling of this element in Books IX and X of *Paradise Lost* I now turn, with misgivings that I hope will be understood.

It will be helpful to begin with clear examples. When Satan, in the form of a serpent, leads Eve to the forbidden tree,

> Hee leading swiftly rowld
> In tangles, and made intricate seem strait,
> To mischief swift. Hope elevates, and joy
> Bright'ns his Crest.

> (IX, 631-34)

His eagerness causes him to move fast, and joy in expected success brightens his crest as a human face may be flushed by pleasurable excitement. "Hope elevates" either the crest, by causing it to stand more erect than usually, or Satan's spirits (and perhaps the posture of his upper body). What is noteworthy here is that the somatic effects of hope and joy are observed from without. We are not told that Satan is aware of them; and very likely he is not, since presumably his attention is focused not on his own feelings but on his purpose.

In contrast Eve's description of the effects of eating the forbidden fruit is aimed at making Adam understand what it feels like to have violated the One Command. "I," she says,

> Have also tasted, and have also found
> Th' effects to correspond, op'ner mine Eyes,
> Dimm erst, dilated spirits, ampler Heart,
> And growing up to Godhead.

> (IX, 874-77)

How much of this has to do with physical sensation is hard to determine.[1] "Op'ner mine Eyes,/ Dimm erst," not only says, but also probably means, that Eve finds her vision sharpened. "Growing up to Godhead" suggests a felt change

[1] Bishop Thomas Newton, in the 1778 revision of his 1749 edition of Milton's poetry, cites a parallel in Tasso's *Aminta* (I, ii): *Sentii mè far di mé stesso maggiore,/ Pien di noua virtu, piena di noua Deitade* (note to IX, 875; borrowed from Thyer).

of status which is continuing as she speaks. "Dilated spirits" and "ampler Heart" are more ambiguous. The former may refer to an enhanced sense of well-being and the latter to increased sympathies, a warmer self-implication in her surroundings; or the spirits may be the animal spirits (which Descartes had recently discussed at length in his *Treatise on the Passions of the Soul*, 1649), and the heart may really be her heart, which a sensation of fullness in the chest makes her imagine to have swelled.

A few lines further down the page the descriptions are more explicitly physical.

> Thus *Eve* with Countnance blithe her storie told;
> But in her Cheek distemper flushing glowd.
> On th' other side, *Adam*, soon as he heard
> The fatal Trespass don by *Eve*, amaz'd,
> Astonied stood and Blank, while horror chill
> Ran through his veins, and all his joints relaxd;
> From his slack hand the Garland wreath'd for *Eve*
> Down dropd, and all the faded Roses shed:
> Speechless he stood and pale, till thus at length
> First to himself he inward silence broke.
>   (IX, 886-95)

Eve's state of mind is shown by a heightened color which contradicts the blandness of her features. Adam turns pale, feels cold, senses a loosening of the joints (one remembers the Homeric description of death in battle, "His knees were loosened"), his hand drops the garland, and for a moment shock prevents him from forming words even in interior monologue. The shock is transmitted to the garland; by a pathetic fallacy the roses fade and drop their petals.

Earlier the effect of Eve's presence on Adam had been quite different.

I from the influence of thy looks receave
Access in every Vertue, in thy sight
More wise, more watchful, stronger, if need were,
Of outward strength; while shame, thou looking on,
Shame to be overcome or over-reacht
Would utmost vigor raise, and rais'd unite.

(IX, 309-14)

Her nearness had had a tonic effect: Adam's muscles had felt stronger, his moral energy greater. ("Vertue" probably includes both the modern sense and the older one of "manliness," "masculinity," qualities which tend, in fallen men, to produce a swagger.) The sense of Eve's softness and gentleness, together with a realization that for the moment he was under her eye, produced a readiness for heroic action, including the sensory watchfulness which would register the need for action.

The admission of such data to Milton's epic verse may not immediately be saluted as a poetic achievement. In recent years the frank description by a poet of his feelings has been execrated: "My heart leaps up when I behold/ A rainbow in the sky"; "I shrieked, and clasped my hands in ecstasy!" Such notations are often crude and may reveal an inability to objectify. Let us, however, distinguish.

The true poetic fault, I suggest, is not in describing the somatic states which accompany strong feelings or intense thought but in describing them at the wrong times, or as a substitute for something which should have been described instead. This often happens on the level of ordinary conversation. A speaker may say, "I never saw anything so horrible in my life!" but fail to make his hearer see the fearful object. For lack of descriptive ability, he interposes his reactions between the hearer and the object and requires, as it were, that the object be taken on faith and that the hearer vibrate in sympathy with his feelings instead of having a direct experience of horror. Such accidental subjectivity, as it may be called, characterizes the writing of many beginners, and the teacher or critic is right to come down hard on it.

The situation is different when the purpose is to describe not the object but the reaction. Wordsworth's poetry is a case in point. In *Tintern Abbey*, for example, some thirteen lines of unusually objective description (lines 10-22) are followed by an explanation in twenty-eight lines of how the poet responded to the view; and in general it is remarkable how little we see in all Wordsworth's nature poetry. Most of the landscape over which the poet bounded like a roe or moved in serene and blessèd mood consists of vague hills and torrents and mists and greenery; we recognize that he is surrounded by it, and in that sense the landscape is real for us, but our attention is primarily on the poet's mind and feelings. In consequence Wordsworth's reputation has fallen, for T. S. Eliot's principle that feelings should be attached to objective correlatives has attained such wide currency that modern critics tend to take it for granted. Wordsworth wished, however, not so much to make people look at nature closely as to awaken in them a realization that benevolent and strengthening influences might be absorbed from it. He assumed acquaintance with natural objects and therefore described the responses which he wished to encourage: responses which were the effect not of close scrutiny like that of Turner and Constable but rather of an empathetic sinking of the consciousness into natural surroundings. To deprecate the subjectivity of his poetry is therefore to deny the legitimacy of his poetic purpose; and such denials should always be made with caution.

Speaking very broadly, what happened was that Romantic poets developed a new kind of self-awareness which, however much it may repel us, marked an intellectual advance of sorts. The subject is too complicated to develop at length;[2] here little more can be said than that a sharp sense of individuality, of separateness from family and culture and nature, emerged only slowly and before the late Renaissance can rarely be glimpsed outside religious meditation, where, indeed, an attempt was often made to obtain relief from it by the establishment of concord with Deity. The history of autobiography offers clear corroboration of this generalization. Both in the psychology of the individual and in the history of the race masses of evidence indicate that a strong awareness of selfhood is achieved only gradually. This may show itself, in literature, in either of two opposite ways: the writer may value individuality, insist on it, and try to win recognition of it from his contemporaries; or, conversely, he may feel it as an intolerable pressure from which an escape must be sought— in Wordsworth, by the reestablishment of oneness with nature, in other writers by other means, including total spiritual union with a beloved of the opposite sex.

A beginning of the long development can be seen in epic, where, however, it was arrested after the publication of *Paradise Lost* because the epic impulse then began to express itself in the subterranean ways described by E. M. W. Tillyard in *The English Epic and Its Background*. I have said that poets have always registered in their verse a somatic element in consciousness. This is true, but in Homer and Virgil the techniques are simple and appear only fitfully. A brief glance at *The Iliad* and *The Aeneid* will suggest how great an advance *Paradise Lost* marks, in this respect, over its most distinguished and influential antecedents.

In *The Iliad* the purely physical strain of battle is sometimes rendered eloquently, as, for example, in a speech by Agamemnon urging immediate attack.

[2] I have covered some of the ground in *English Autobiography: Its Emergence, Materials, and Form*, Berkeley: University of California Press, 1954, especially Chapter 1.

ἱδρώσει μέν τευ τελαμὼν ἀμφὶ στήθεσφιν
ἀσπίδος ἀμφιβρότης, περὶ δ' ἔγχεϊ χεῖρα καμεῖται ·
ἱδρώσει δέ τευ ἵππος ἐΰξοον ἅρμα τιταίνων.

(Wet with sweat about the breast of many a man shall be
the baldric of his sheltering shield, and about the spear
shall his hand grow weary, and wet with sweat shall a
man's horse be, as he tugs at the polished car. *Iliad* II,
388-90.)[3]

In this passage selected bodily sensations are not only described in men but are recognized empathetically in horses.
At this sort of thing Homer is very good, though he seldom
pauses to elaborate, and the description of an injury regularly substitutes for a description of the pain it has caused
("He was smitten on the right breast beside the nipple; and
clean through his shoulder went the spear of bronze, and he
fell"—IV, 480-82, p. 189); "So the stubborn bronze shore off
his tongue at its root, and the spear-point came out by the
base of the chin. Then he fell . . ."—v, 292-93, p. 217). The
somatic accompaniments of strong emotions, on the other
hand—fear, rage, frustration, and dread, not to mention such
less military feelings as love—are more briefly registered:
"with rage was his black heart wholly filled, and his eyes
were like blazing fire" (I, 103-104, p. 11); "To them then
Dolon made answer, and his limbs trembled beneath him"
(x, 390, p. 415).

This is of course not to say that Homer is unable to make
us empathize. We sympathize strongly with Hector's wife,
Andromache, when she urges her husband not to go forth
from the city.

My father verily goodly Achilles slew. . . . And the seven
brothers that were mine in our halls, all these on the selfsame

[3] Trans. A. T. Murray, *Homer: The Iliad*, Cambridge, Mass.: Harvard
University Press, 1960, I, 79.

173

day entered into the house of Hades. . . . In her father's halls
Artemis the archer slew [my mother]. Nay, Hector, thou
art to me father and queenly mother, thou art brother, and
thou art my stalwart husband. Come now, have pity, and
remain here on the wall, lest thou make thy child an orphan
and thy wife a widow. (VI, 414-32, p. 293)

We are touched also by the dread of Hector's son at the horse-
haired crest of his father's helmet (VI, 466-70, p. 297), and by
much else. But the somatic element in all this is relatively
small, as can be seen if we set side by side similar passages
from Milton and Homer.

In Book IX of *Paradise Lost*, after in his turn eating of the
fruit, Adam is strongly aroused by Eve's beauty. The passage
will bear quotation at some length.

> As with new Wine intoxicated both
> They swim in mirth, and fansie that they feel
> Divinitie within them breeding wings
> Wherewith to scorn the Earth: but that false Fruit
> Farr other operation first displaid,
> Carnal desire enflaming; hee on *Eve*
> Began to cast lascivious Eyes, shee him
> As wantonly repaid; in Lust they burne:
> Till *Adam* thus 'gan *Eve* to dalliance move. . . .
> But come, so well refresht, now let us play,
> As meet is, after such delicious Fare;
> For never did thy Beautie since the day
> I saw thee first and wedded thee, adornd
> With all perfections, so enflame my sense
> With ardor to enjoy thee, fairer now
> Then ever, bountie of this vertuous Tree.

So said he, and forbore not glance or toy
Of amorous intent, well understood
Of *Eve*, whose Eye darted contagious Fire.
Her hand he seis'd, and to a shadie bank,
Thick overhead with verdant roof imbowr'd
He led her nothing loath; Flours were the Couch,
Pansies, and Violets, and Asphodel,
And Hyacinth, Earths freshest softest lap.
There they thir fill of Love and Loves disport
Took largely, of thir mutual guilt the Seale,
The solace of thir sin, till dewie sleep
Oppressd them, wearied with thir amorous play.

(IX, 1,008-16, 1,027-45)

The equivalent in *The Iliad*, so close as to be a probable
"source," appears in Book III. Paris has been snatched from
death at the hand of Menelaus by Aphrodite and returned
magically to his chamber; his wife Helen is now brought
there, against her will, by the same goddess and chides him
before beginning slightly to relent. Paris's reply runs as follows. (This time I will relegate the Greek to a note.)

Then Paris made answer, and spake to her, saying:
"Chide not my heart, lady, with hard words of reviling.
For this present hath Menelaus vanquished me with
Athene's aid, but another time shall I vanquish him; on our
side too there be gods. But come, let us take our joy,
couched together in love; for never yet hath desire so encompassed my soul—nay, not when at the first I snatched
thee from lovely Lacedaemon and sailed with thee on my
sea-faring ships, and on the isle of Cranaë had dalliance
with thee on the couch of love—as now I love thee, and
sweet desire layeth hold of me."

He spake, and led the way to the couch, and with him followed his wife.

Thus the twain were couched upon the corded bed; but the son of Atreus . . . (III, 437-49, pp. 149, 151)[4]

Although there may be readers who prefer the Homeric passage to the Miltonic, as there are readers who prefer the Biblical narrative of the creation to Milton's, comparison shows very clearly how much more than Homer Milton can render directly.

In Homer the description of a somatic state, that of erotic passion, is virtually limited to the two phrases, "Never yet hath desire so encompassed my soul" and "Now I love thee, and sweet desire layeth hold of me." But this is no more than to name the emotion and is far from detailing its physical concomitants—quickened breath, aroused senses, the excitation of nerve-endings in the skin, and the rest. If we understand, and perhaps to a degree empathetically share, Paris's eagerness, the reason is that we have had some direct experience of erotic passion. In another poet, the adjective in the phrase

[4] Τὴν δὲ Πάρις μύθοισιν ἀμειβόμενος προσέειπε·
"μή με, γύναι, χαλεποῖσιν ὀνείδεσι θυμὸν ἔνιπτε.
νῦν μὲν γὰρ Μενέλαος ἐνίκησεν σὺν Ἀθήνῃ,
κεῖνον δ' αὖτις ἐγώ· πάρα γὰρ θεοί εἰσι καὶ ἡμῖν.
ἀλλ' ἄγε δὴ φιλότητι τραπείομεν εὐνηθέντε·
οὐ γάρ πώ ποτέ μ' ὧδέ γ' ἔρως φρένας ἀμφεκάλυψεν,
οὐδ' ὅτε σε πρῶτον Λακεδαίμονος ἐξ ἐρατεινῆς
ἔπλεον ἁρπάξας ἐν ποντοπόροισι νέεσσι,
νήσῳ δ' ἐν Κραναῇ ἐμίγην φιλότητι καὶ εὐνῇ,
ὥς σεο νῦν ἔραμαι καί με γλυκὺς ἵμερος αἱρεῖ."
Ἦ ῥα, καὶ ἄρχε λέχοσδε κιών· ἅμα δ' εἵπετ' ἄκοιτις.
Τὼ μὲν ἄρ' ἐν τρητοῖσι κατεύνασθεν λεχέεσσιν,
Ἀτρεΐδης δ' . . .

Another parallel is with the passage (*Iliad*, XIV, 153-351, especially 313-28 and 346-51) in which Hera, wishing to distract Zeus's attention from the battle, adorns herself to enflame his senses. P.L. IX, 1,039-41 reflects *Iliad* XIV, 346-51 strikingly; but the *somatic* notations are again minimal, and the union is prepared for by Hera and is not spontaneous, as in P.L. IX and *Iliad* III.

"lovely Lacedaemon" might be a transference from the desirable woman to a setting in which the act of love had been enjoyed previously. Here it is not, or is so only at a secondary level, for Lacedaemon is lovely (ἐρατεινή) in the same way that Achilles is "god-like" (δῖος) or "swift-footed" (πόδας ὠκύς) and would be equally lovely in another quite different context. In "snatched" there is a suggestion of the pressure under which the first fruition was accomplished; but on the whole, wonderfully effective as the passage is, we can note its "objectivity," its lack of the acute and almost painful self-awareness which was often to characterize poetry written after the sense of individuality had progressed further. Paris says scarcely more than is necessary to communicate his desire; and neither the erotic climax nor its aftermath interests the poet sufficiently to invite lingering.

The Milton passage, although pre-Romantic, is more sensitively observant. After eating the fruit, Adam and Eve

> swim in mirth, and fansie that they feel
> Divinitie within them breeding wings
> Wherewith to scorn the Earth . . .

This is relevant to the love-union because preparatory for it. The first effect of the sin is a bodily euphoria which manifests itself as a pleasure so keen that it requires a physical outlet in gesture and perhaps in laughter. The expansiveness of the mood produces a physical "elevation" which feels like winged flight above the earth: the couple "fansie that they feel/ Divinitie within them breeding wings." Alas, the sensation is evanescent and is succeeded by an all too earthly drive.

> that false Fruit
> Farr other operation first displaid,
> Carnal desire enflaming . . .

Adam casts "lascivious Eyes" on Eve (we know the look); "shee him/ As wantonly repaid; in Lust they burne." The authenticity of burning as a metaphor of erotic passion is attested, among many other phrases, by the term "heat" as applied to animals.

> For never did thy Beautie since the day
> I saw thee first and wedded thee, adornd
> With all perfections, so enflame my sense
> With ardor to enjoy thee, fairer now
> Then ever . . .

Eve's physical attractions are now more irresistibly enticing than ever before, as Helen's were to Paris; but Adam's expression of his lust is more flattering to its object, for he imputes the cause to Eve instead of focusing upon himself (Paris had said, "Never yet hath desire so encompassed my soul"). Moreover, the senses, quite accurately, are said to be abnormally enflamed—a somatic notation missing from Homer's description. Thus speaking, Adam "forebore not glance or toy/ Of amorous intent," which were reciprocated by Eve, "whose Eye darted contagious Fire." Adam seizes Eve's hand (there is no actual physical contact in Homer), and on a flowery couch "They thir fill of Love and Love's disport/ Took largely . . ./ . . . till dewie sleep/ Oppressd them, wearied with thir amorous play." As applied to Eve, the phrase "took thir fill of Love" is almost shockingly apt, like the Freudian description of Earthly Paradise which C. S. Lewis has noticed. After the consummation, like other lovers they are "oppressd," weighed down, by sleep and weariness. Much of what we infer from Homer is thus directly shown by Milton. Whichever of the two passages we may prefer as art (and I suspect that doctrinal precommitments will inevitably influence our judgment), Milton's is much more faithful to the post-Renaissance consciousness.

A comparison with Virgil yields somewhat different findings. The most nearly parallel passages are those which concern Dido's relations with Aeneas, though the account of the physical union is disappointingly casual ("To the same cave come Dido and the Trojan chief," *speluncam Dido dux et Troianus eandem/ deveniunt*, IV, 165-66).[5] By signs Earth and Juno give their approval; but of Aeneas's physical or mental state nothing at all is said, and of Dido's we are told only that she is no longer "swayed by fair show or fair fame, no more does she dream of a secret love: she calls it marriage and with that name veils her sin" (170-72). Dido's passion when Aeneas is about to desert her is described in unusual detail, however, and offers an excellent basis for contrast.

In large part Virgil's descriptions focus on rage. "Helpless in mind she rages, and all aflame raves through the city" (IV, 300-301); she weeps (314), looks at Aeneas askance, "turning her eyes to and fro" (362-63); incensed, she feels herself carried away by fury (376), "breaks off her speech midway and flees in anguish from the light" (388-89), and at length swoons (391). Later she utters sighs (409), weeps again (413), yearns for rest and release from her frenzy (433), prays for death (451), is filled with foreboding (464-65), is overcome by anguish (474), becomes pale (499), and is unable to sleep (529-30). Up to this point the physical manifestations have been portrayed not from within but from without—any spectator could have observed them—or have consisted merely of named affections like helplessness of mind, frenzy, anguish,

---

[5] The citations are from the Loeb edition of Virgil, London: William Heinemann Ltd., 1950, Vol. I, with an English translation by H. Rushton Fairclough. Quoted phrases in English are from Fairclough unless otherwise annotated; the line citations are to the Latin. Only Book IV of the *Aeneid* is involved.

yearning, and foreboding, none of which are given specific somatic associations. To judge from Fairclough's rendering, the very next sentence includes something like somatic perception: "Her pangs redouble, and her love, swelling up, surges afresh, as she heaves with a mighty tide of passion" (531-32). The swelling might be an authentic physical sensation (as the heaving of course is); but it is not, for the strict sense of the Latin is "Her cares redouble, and her love, rising again, rages, and she tosses in the fierce heat of anger" (*ingeminant curae, rursusque resurgens/ saevit amor, magnoque irarum fluctuat aestu*). The heat is a metaphor for actual sensation, but it had long been traditional and was not a technical innovation by Virgil, and *resurgens*, "rising again," may mean little more than "regaining prominence." The heat appears elsewhere, as in "rouses the varied heats of anger" (564—my translation); for the rest, the description again falls back chiefly on outward manifestations of disturbance. On the whole, the treatment is dramatic rather than analytic. The descriptive passages resemble stage directions for an actress who would speak Dido's lines in a voice expressive of anguish, yearning, helplessness, foreboding, and so on and would perform the actions that are indicated with facial expressions that she thought appropriate. For my taste, I confess, the episode is a good deal too strained, a good deal too operatic. Whether or not it deserves its critical repute, however, it stands only a little nearer than Homer to the registering of somatic perceptions. Much has intervened between Homer and Virgil, including drama; but the Roman poet continues to observe passion from without instead of perceiving it intimately from inside a state of mind into which he has projected himself by an act of sympathetic imagination.

With this introduction we may proceed to look, in turn, at other parts of Book IX and then at relevant passages of

Book X. And first at Satan, of whom Milton disapproved
with all the strength of his powerful intellect without losing
the ability to understand him and even, at times, to identify
with him not only emotionally but also physically.

Since Milton attempted to follow ancient precedent, it is
not surprising that he sometimes wrote like his models.

> full of anguish driv'n,
> The space of sev'n continu'd Nights he rode
> With darkness.
>
> (IX, 62-64)

The anguish is like Dido's and is named, like hers, together
with the action it inspired. Soon, however, the emotion becomes more specific.

> the more I see
> Pleasures about me, so much more I feel
> Torment within me, as from the hateful siege
> Of contraries; all good to mee becomes
> Bane, and in Heav'n much worse would be my state.
>
> (IX, 119-23)

Here we are shown the poisoning of perception. The attrac-
tiveness of Satan's surroundings awakens "Torment," which
is a state of mind so oppressive that it affects not only the
mind but also the nerves. "All good to mee becomes/ Bane":
"Bane" means "a cause of death," and especially "deadly
poison"; the perception of good evokes a welling up of hatred
which is felt as self-destructive. The only relief to be hoped
for is the infection of others with the same virus.

> Nor hope to be my self less miserable
> By what I seek, but others to make such
> As I, though thereby worse to me redound:

For onely in destroying I find ease
To my relentless thoughts.

(IX, 126-30)

The pressure of hatred is so strong that relief can be obtained only from smashing things. The psychosomatic state is known to us all, although most of us, being less thoroughly evil than Satan, are satisfied with the breaking of a vase or the slamming down of a tool.

As Satan plots his seduction of the Parents he must elude the vigilance of the "flaming Ministers" (IX, 156) God has placed in the Garden; so he first takes the form of a black mist and later enters the body of the serpent. As mist, he "pries" in "every Bush and Brake," (IX, 159-60), a verb which suggests the sending out of exploratory tentacles. Once involved in the "mazie foulds" (IX, 161) of the serpent, he knows he will be "constraind/ Into a Beast, and mixt with bestial slime" in such a way as to "incarnate and imbrute" an essence which had once aspired to Deity (IX, 164-67). The anticipatory awareness of a repugnant physical envelope for the spirit is here quite explicit. Later, when he sees Eve among the roses, he reacts, in a famous simile,

> As one who long in populous City pent,
> Where Houses thick and Sewers annoy the Aire,
> Forth issuing on a Summers Morn to breathe
> Among the pleasant Villages and Farmes
> Adjoind, from each thing met conceaves delight,
> The smell of Grain, or tedded Grass, or Kine,
> Or Dairie, each rural sight, each rural sound;
> If chance with Nymphlike step fair Virgin pass,
> What pleasing seemd, for her now pleases more,
> Shee most . . .

(IX, 445-54)

In the city there has been a sense of crowding; in the country one "breathes," expands one's chest to savor the agreeable odors which have replaced the stench of sewers. The effect is a general enhancing of sensory awareness, so that the vision of an attractive young woman increases the pleasure obtained from the senses.

What follows is even more remarkable. First, however, we note that Satan's impression of Eve's figure is not only as something "Angelic," but also as something "more soft, and Feminine" (IX, 458)—a tactile perception, though experienced at a distance.

> Her graceful Innocence, her every Aire
> Of gesture or lest action overawd
> His Malice, and with rapin sweet bereav'd
> His fierceness of the fierce intent it brought:
> That space the Evil one abstracted stood
> From his own evil, and for the time remaind
> Stupidly good, of enmitie disarmd,
> Of guile, of hate, of envie, of revenge.
>
> (IX, 459-66)

As much as, perhaps more than, any other passage of the entire epic, this excerpt shows the poet sinking himself into an attitude, and even a personality, alien to his own. Eve's beauty and innocence, by an act of forcible seizure (*rapina*), remove from Satan's fierce hatred of good things his baleful purpose of doing harm, so that for a moment there is a quasi-physical separation ("abstracted" means "drawn away") between active evil and the father of evil. "Disarmd," or deprived by a superior moral force, of guile, hate, and envy, Satan remains "Stupidly good." I wish one could be certain that "stupid" here has its modern meaning and not merely the etymological one, "struck silent" (from *stupēre*), for the word would then indicate that the poet so completely shares

Satan's bad purpose as to disapprove, for a single wonderful
moment, of his villain's susceptibility to lovely innocence. In
any event, what Milton has attempted to describe in the passage is an emptying, a draining of both moral and physical
energy which leaves Satan powerless and gaping.

In an instant the Devil comes to himself.

> then soon
> Fierce hate he recollects, and all his thoughts
> Of mischief, gratulating, thus excites.
>   Thoughts, whither have ye led me, with what sweet
> Compulsion thus transported to forget
> What hither brought us, hate, not love . . .
>   (IX, 470-75)

Remembering his enmity toward the woman, he tries to return to the spiritual and physical position from which he has
been "transported," carried away, by "sweet Compulsion," a
set of energies which have invaded him from without. He
can understand what has happened only on one hypothesis:
"so much hath Hell debas't, and paine/ Infeebl'd me, to what
I was in Heav'n" (IX, 487-88). Again the somatic element in
the experience is made specific. Next, in another extraordinary
passage, he speaks again of Eve:

> Shee fair, divinely fair, fit Love for Gods,
> Not terrible, though terrour be in Love
> And beautie, not approacht by stronger hate,
> Hate stronger, under shew of Love well feignd.
>   (IX, 489-92)

He is trying to persuade himself of what he wants to believe:
that his momentary stupefaction must have been a pretense
which has only intensified his hate.[6] "Though terrour be in
Love" is an acute observation which it is surprising Satan

---

[6] More explicitly, the speech has to do with the coming interview.

should make, and it once more designates an emotion strong enough to take possession of the whole mind-body. From this point the somatic notations continue to be sensitive. Satan approaches Eve "With tract oblique," as one who "feard/ To interrupt" (ix, 510-12); and when he must reply to Eve's objection that "of this Tree we may not taste nor touch" (ix, 651), he first wriggles passionately, like an excited animal ("as to passion mov'd,/ Fluctuats disturbd, yet comely," ix, 667-68), and then collects himself, "while each part,/ Motion, each act won audience ere the tongue" (ix, 673-74). But we have no space to dwell longer on Satan and must turn back to the Parents.

It is important to observe that we are not concerned only with the visual, auditory, olfactory, and other sensory images already familiar to criticism, although some of these are relevant and deserve notice. Somatic imagery includes much more—for example, concern over the behavior of the sex organs.

> Cover me ye Pines,
> Ye Cedars, with innumerable boughs
> Hide me . . .
>   devise
> What best may for the present serve to hide
> The Parts of each from other . . .
> Those middle parts, that this new commer, Shame,
> There sit not, and reproach us as unclean.
>   (ix, 1,088-98)

Not much should be made of this detail. It was imposed on Milton by a theological tradition already fully articulated by St. Augustine (*The City of God*, Book xiv, Chapter 17ff.) and implicit in *Genesis* itself. Moreover, the poetry here is not especially taut, perhaps because Milton himself, for all his hyperacute sensitivity to feminine beauty, was not much afflicted by this particular anxiety. Elsewhere the somatic awareness is more intimately the poet's—often expressed, to be sure, in terms suggested by a contemporary psychology, but nonetheless indicative of a total involvement in the mythical incidents.

The quarrel which followed the assumption of clothing is a case in point.

> Thus fenc't, and as they thought, thir shame in part
> Coverd, but not at rest or ease of Mind,
> They sate them down to weep, nor onely Teares
> Raind at thir Eyes, but high Winds worse within
> Began to rise, high Passions, Anger, Hate,
> Mistrust, Suspicion, Discord, and shook sore
> Thir inward State of Mind, calme Region once
> And full of Peace, now tost and turbulent:
> For Understanding rul'd not, and the Will
> Heard not her lore, both in subjection now
> To sensual Appetite, who from beneath
> Usurping over sovran Reason claimd
> Superior sway.
>
> (IX, 1,119-31)

"From beneath. . . ." The mind, formerly peaceful, is now disturbed by impulses coming from a source that is lower both hierarchically and physically, and these "over sovran Reason claimd/ Superior sway." The effect is tears and gusts— "high Winds"—of passion: anger, hate, mistrust, suspicion, discord. Appetite, which has its origin in the body, destroys the autonomy of the will.

The sequel can be followed in Book X, to which we shall turn in a moment. In the meantime it may be observed that sensitivity to the body is pervasive in the epic.

> Thus saying, from her Husbands hand her hand

Soft she withdrew, and like a Wood-Nymph light
Oread or *Dryad*, or of *Delia's* Traine,
Betook her to the Groves, but *Delia's* self
In gate surpassd and Goddess-like deport.

(IX, 385-89)

The withdrawal of the hand has been commented on as a
symbol of spiritual alienation, which of course it is; but the
word "Soft," besides meaning "slowly" or "gently," also hints
at a tactile sensation, and the description of gait is dwelt on
too lovingly to have only the designatory significance of
Virgil's *vera incessu patuit dea* ("The true goddess reveals
herself by her gait"—*Aeneid*, 1, 405). Milton is watching his
naked Eve with a delight tinged by sexuality. Or, in another
passage, Eve's tending of flowers before the insinuating approach of the serpent is described in such a way as to show
her empathetic recognition of strain in the plants themselves.

oft stooping to support
Each Flour of slender stalk, whose head though gay
Carnation, Purple, Azure, or spect with Gold,
Hung drooping unsustaind, them she upstaies
Gently with Mirtle band, mindless the while,
Her self, though fairest unsupported Flour,
From her best prop so farr, and storm so nigh.

(IX, 427-33)

In the last two lines the poet transfers to Eve herself the
weakness she is attempting to remedy in the flowers. Milton
sees her as frail, not only spiritually and intellectually but
also physically.

When the Son judges the pair mental confusion affects
physical behavior.

Love was not in thir looks, either to God
Or to each other, but apparent guilt,

187

And shame, and perturbation, and despaire,
Anger, and obstinacie, and hate, and guile.
Whence *Adam* faultring long, thus answerd brief.
I heard thee in the Garden, and of thy voice
Affraid, being naked, hid my self.

(x, 111-17)

Eve speaks only briefly, "with shame nigh overwhelmd" and "abasht" (x, 159-61). Later, Adam foresees that their descendants will recognize by "feeling" the bodily evils for which the ancestors are responsible:

Who of all Ages to succeed, but feeling
The evil on him brought by mee, will curse
My Head, Ill fare our Ancestor impure,
For this we may thank *Adam*.

(x, 733-36)

He experiences in his own body the physical changes brought on by his transgression and yearns for the peace of extinction.

why do I overlive,
Why am I mockt with death, and length'nd out
To deathless pain? how gladly would I meet
Mortalitie my sentence, and be Earth
Insensible, how glad would lay me down
As in my Mothers lap! there I should rest
And sleep secure . . .

(x, 773-79)

The taint will be communicated to his progeny: "But from mee what can proceed,/ But all corrupt?" (x, 824-25) He abandons himself to a despair which expresses itself not only in words but also in posture:

On the ground
Outstretcht he lay, on the cold ground, and oft

Curs'd his Creation, Death as oft accus'd
Of tardie execution.

(x, 850-53)

The implication of the body in the sin has led to a total retrogression.

Relief is at hand, but it must be attained through a quarrel in which Adam recriminates bitterly. Eve's treachery has been so great that it could have been expected only of a being whose body was less divine:

> nothing wants, but that thy shape,
> Like his, and colour Serpentine may shew
> Thy inward fraud, to warn all Creatures from thee
> Henceforth; least that too heav'nly form, pretended
> To hellish falshood, snare them.

(x, 869-73)

She is "a Rib/ Crooked by nature, bent, as now appears,/ More to the part sinister . . ./ Well if thrown out" (x, 884-87), a "fair defect/ Of Nature" (x, 891-92). The lack of concord between Eve's body and her behavior was unexpected and still evokes wonder. Eve, in reply, testifies remorse by physical action as well as by words.

> He added not, and from her turnd, but *Eve*
> Not so repulst, with Tears that ceas'd not flowing,
> And tresses all disorderd, at his feet
> Fell humble, and imbracing them, besaught
> His peace, and thus proceeded in her plaint.
> . . . thy suppliant
> I beg, and clasp thy knees . . .

(x, 909-18)

Adam, she says, is her "onely strength and stay" (x, 921). From the present wallowing and self-commiserating husband

189

she can draw no help; but the spectacle of her distress recalls him to himself.

> soon his heart relented
> Towards her, his life so late and sole delight,
> Now at his feet submissive in distress,
> Creature so faire his reconcilement seeking . . .
> As one disarmd, his anger all he lost.
>
> (x, 940-45)

They embark on a discussion of the "woful Race" to be brought into the world through their "Loines" (983-84). Eve counsels abstinence from the marital act to prevent conception but realizes that the flesh will perhaps make demands too powerful to be resisted:

> But if thou judge it hard and difficult,
> Conversing, looking, loving, to abstain
> From Loves due Rites, Nuptial embraces sweet,
> And with desire to languish without hope,
>   . . . which would be miserie
> And torment less then none of what we dread . . .
>
> (x, 992-98)

The safest recourse will perhaps be suicide. Adam, however, recalls the prophecy that the seed of the woman will crush the head of the serpent—another physical notation—recalls the "mild/ And gracious temper" (x, 1,046-47) of the Son as he rendered judgment, and counsels a repentance whose sincerity will be avouched by bodily gesture. Let us, he says, in the place where the judgment was spoken,

>   prostrate fall
> Before him reverent, and there confess
> Humbly our faults, and pardon beg, with tears
> Watering the ground, and with our sighs the Air

Frequenting, sent from hearts contrite, in sign
Of sorrow unfeignd, and humiliation meek.
                    (x, 1,087-92)

With the performance of this act the plot curves upward.
Hereafter the parents will again be able to stand erect, though
with a bashfulness and self-distrust foreign to their prelap-
sarian bearing.

In other strands of Books IX and X the somatic awareness
reveals itself clearly. A connection of the body with the mind
underlies the redemptive mission of the Son: "thou knowst,/
Whoever judg'd, the worst on mee must light" (x, 72-73).
The sin of the first parents must be punished in a human
body assumed by the Second Person of the Godhead. In a long
and painful meditation, Adam decides that the sentence of
death pronounced on his body must be executed also on his
spirit: "All of me then shall die" (x, 792). Satan and the other
devils are punished physically for a sin which had been es-
sentially of the spirit; and we are told how the punishment
feels.

> His Visage drawn he felt to sharp and spare,
> His Armes clung to his Ribs, his Leggs entwining
> Each other, till supplanted down he fell
> A monstrous Serpent on his Belly prone,
>   . . . he would have spoke,
> But hiss for hiss returnd with forked tongue
> To forked tongue, for now were all transformd
> Alike.
>   (x, 511-20)

When the remaining devils, who have been waiting outside
Pandaemonium, see what has happened,

>   horror on them fell,
> And horrid sympathie; for what they saw,

They felt themselves now changing.

(x, 539-41)

The delusive fruit which has sprung up in Hell turns in
their mouths to ashes, which they "With spattering noise
rejected," so that they "writh'd thir jaws/ With soot and
cinders filld" (x, 567-70). Across not only the whole universe
but also an almost illimitable Chaos, Sin feels, at the moment
the original transgression is completed, a new strength rising,
wings growing, and a new dominion given her (x, 243-44);
Death snuffs with delight the "mortal change on Earth" (x,
272-73) and upturns "His Nostril wide into the murkie Air,/
Sagacious of his Quarrey from so farr" (x, 280-81). Chaos,
abstraction though he is, resents the bridge built through his
territories, "And with rebounding surge the barrs assaild,/
That scornd his indignation" (x, 417-18). Arrived on earth,
Death is all appetite, all *soma*:

Alike is Hell, or Paradise, or Heaven,
There best, where most with ravin I may meet;
Which here, though plenteous, all too little seems
To stuff this Maw, this vast unhide-bound Corps.

(x, 598-601)

The "draff and filth" which God has called them to lick up
(x, 630) is the product of Man's "polluting Sin," which has
shed a "taint" on what had previously been pure (x, 631-32).
What is spiritual is closely bound up with the physical. And
there are other alterations of earthly economy. The earth shifts
its axis, or the sun alters its path, so that the earth may be
affected "with cold and heat/ Scarce tollerable" (x, 653-54).
Animal life, hitherto peaceful, becomes voracious:

Beast now with Beast gan warr, and Fowle with Fowle,
And Fish with Fish; to graze the Herb all leaving,
Devourd each other.

(x, 710-12)

Everywhere the realms of the mental and of the physical interpenetrate, so that modifications of one induce changes in the other.

Why is this so? A part of the answer is in the subject itself, which took its essential form at a time when the two realms had not yet been sharply discriminated. More than this is involved, however, for in such a poet as Du Bartas the interpenetration is less marked. Difficult as it is to discern the boundary between mere sensory imagery and a consciousness of the body as such (I am aware that some of the illustrations given above may seem irrelevant to readers who question the *poet*'s somatic involvement), the evidence is sufficiently clear that *Paradise Lost* takes astonishing account of the body. That the poem is rich in concepts has always been recognized; but that it is also highly physical, *somatic*, may come as a surprise. Believing as he did in the primacy of the will, Milton would have rejected with indignation the claim of a group of present-day American critics that "the guts are always right." Yet the persistent mingling of percept with affect in his narrative makes him, in this respect as in others, curiously modern. Perhaps he benefited from his materialism, which tended, whether he realized the implication or not, to call into question the traditional psychology that fractured the mind-body unity into a number of autonomous "faculties." Whatever the cause, however, emotion in *Paradise Lost* is not of the mind or spirit only but involves the total being.

CHAPTER IX

....

AFFECT AND PERCEPT

ON THE MOUNT OF

SPECULATION

The last two books of *Paradise Lost* have not been among
the most admired. This is not to be wondered at, for the
poet had several difficulties to confront. The action within
the epic's real imaginative universe is over, and what remains
is to be foreseen rather than experienced directly. Michael
and Adam stand on "a Hill/ Of Paradise the highest" (xi,
377-78) and consider at a distance both of space and of time
events which lie in the narrative future. At best they are
spectators, not participants; but in Book XII Adam no longer
sees what is to happen and only hears the archangel's description. Also, the scope of the books is excessive. According to
Archbishop Ussher's chronology (*Annales Veteris Testamenti*,
1650-54), 4,004 years stretched from the Fall described in
Milton's ninth book to the Incarnation of Christ, and 1,667
years from the Incarnation to the date of publication; and in
XII, 537-51, Michael looks ahead from the poet's present to
the Second Judgment, which Milton had thought impending
in 1641[1] but had subsequently had to postdate. As the plan was
to develop, all this enormous stretch of human calamities was
to be summarized in the 1,077 lines from XI, 376 to XII, 551.

[1] "—at that day when thou the Eternall and shortly-expected King shalt
open the Clouds to judge the severall Kingdomes of the World." *Of Reforma-
tion Touching Church-Discipline*, in *The Works of John Milton*, New York:
The Columbia University Press, 1931-1938, Vol. iii, Part One, 78.

Inevitably, compression interferes with immediacy. Everybody knows that a summary of a novel is less vivid than the novel. Besides all this, the reader may now be tiring and eager to get to the end. Milton is not easy reading, and the typical undergraduate, at least, is likely either not to be enchanted with literature or to be impatient to move on to the next waiting masterpiece. Even scholars are not proof against fatigue. Like the undergraduate they sense that the essential drama is over; and they are affected by an interpretative tradition which puts the emphasis elsewhere.

The tradition, in fact, is generally unenthusiastic about the two books and in part frankly hostile. C. S. Lewis thought the books offered an "untransmuted lump of futurity" in which the writing is "curiously bad"; and he quotes Johnson's remark on ballads, that "the story cannot possibly be told in a manner that shall make less impression on the mind."[2] According to Bishop Newton, writing in 1749, "The reader probably may have observed that these two last books fall short of the sublimity and majesty of the rest." He adds, defensively, that "so likewise do the two last books of the *Iliad*, and for the same reason, because the subject is of a different kind from that of the foregoing ones. The subject of these two last books of the Paradise Lost is history rather than poetry."[3] Recently attempts have been made to justify the books as logically necessary to Milton's plan.[4] Here we shall seek to discover whether in them Milton continued to perceive effectively and to impregnate the poetry with feeling. For the sake of orderliness, an effort will be made to keep the two halves of the discussion separate.

Before beginning, we may notice that for Milton and his

[2] Lewis, *Preface to Paradise Lost*, p. 129.

[3] Thomas Newton, ed., *Paradise Lost: A Poem, in Twelve Books*, London, 1749, note to XII, 648.

[4] Joseph Summers, in the final chapter of *The Muse's Method: An Introduction to Paradise Lost*, Cambridge, Mass.: Harvard University Press, 1962, has

contemporaries there could hardly have been any alternative to describing postlapsarian history at considerable length. For one thing, the frightful consequences of the Fall were written large in it, and the magnitude of the sin could be brought home to men's bosoms only by relating all human sufferings to the rind of one apple tasted. *This* is the evil for which man and not God is responsible. Moreover, the epic was traditionally a protracted literary work. The *Iliad* ran to 15,693 lines, the *Odyssey* to 12,210, the *Aeneid* to 9,896, *Orlando Furioso* to 38,632, the *Gerusalemme Liberata* to 15,280, the *Faerie Queene* to 34,596. To the end of Book X, *Paradise Lost* extended only to 9,015 lines. Finally, and not least important, rhetoric, to which poetry was still closely linked in the minds of educated men, consisted in very large part of techniques by which *copia*, or abundance, could be achieved. From boyhood, probably, Milton had been trained to hold his reader's (or auditor's) attention for an appropriately long time on whatever important statements he might make. It was unthinkable that the effects of the Parents' sin should be brushed off by a simple generalization ("—and that is why men have suffered ever since"). What was important had, almost automatically, by a prepared scholarly reflex, to be made impressive.

What this meant in practice is suggested by the *De Utraque Verborum ac Rerum Copia* of Erasmus, which was dedicated to John Colet, the founder of St. Paul's School, and which went through some eighty-five editions between 1512 and 1536 and perhaps 150 to 160 European editions in the sixteenth century. There is space for only one expanded illustration. Suppose a schoolboy wishes to expatiate properly on the notion that "He lost everything through excess." This idea, Erasmus points out, "may be developed by enumerating a great many kinds of possessions, and by setting forth various

---

written nobly of Books XI and XII. I find his discussion admirable but view the books here from a different angle of vision.

ways of losing property." The word "everything" can be expanded as follows:

Whatever had come by inheritance from father or mother, whatever had come by the death of other relatives, whatever had been added from his wife's dowry, which was not at all mean, whatever had accrued from bequests (and considerable had accrued), whatever he had received from the liberality of his prince, whatever private property he had procured, all money, military equipment, clothes, estates, fields, together with farms and herds, in short, everything, whether movable or real estate, and finally even his immediate household property . . .

In this way the significance of "everything" can be suggested (and the schoolboy can keep talking or writing instead of grinding prematurely to a halt). As for "lost through excess," we may render it as

in a short time he so consumed, wasted, and devoured in foulest passion for harlots, in daily banquets, in sumptuous entertainments, nightly drinking bouts, low taverns, delicacies, perfumes, dice, and gaming that what remained to him would not equal a farthing.[5]

Similarly, "He has finished his education" can be developed "by recounting one by one the individual disciplines—every field of learning." "Endowed with all the gifts of nature and fortune" can be expanded by enumerating "the individual physical advantages, then one by one the gifts of intellect and of character, lastly, family, wealth, country, success and whatever good fortune commonly brings." "He was drenched" can be saved from standing stupidly alone by specifying all the

[5] The example has been taken from Desiderius Erasmus of Rotterdam, *On Copia of Words and Ideas*, trans. Donald B. King and H. David Rix, Milwaukee, Wis.: Marquette University Press, 1963, p. 43.

parts of the body which became wet, from the victim's "topmost hair" down to "the very bottom of his shoe."[6]

The technique was not without practical usefulness. Everyone who has taught freshman composition knows the stubborn tendency of untrained writers, after producing such a sentence as "The aim of a liberal education is to develop the mind," to add next something entirely different, like "It also helps the student to earn a better living." At this rate, the completion of an assigned five-hundred word essay is next to impossible, since it requires the thinking up of as many subjects for separate essays as the total number of sentences. Evidently medieval and Renaissance school masters had encountered a similar tendency. They met it by developing an elaborate method by which literary constipation could be transformed to a kind of diarrhea. Rhetorical training may thus not improbably have contributed to the gargantuan size of many treatises and poems. In this pedagogical context, which encouraged also the amassing of compendia of every conceivable kind of knowledge, Milton's use of only 1,077 lines to summarize the events of 5,671 years plus whatever additional time might intervene between 1667 and the Millennium shows commendable restraint. Du Bartas' *La Premiere Sepmaine* had used 6,494 lines to cover the ground over which Milton swooped in the 640 lines of his seventh book. We may therefore, I think, accept the size of Books XI and XII as modest.

At the beginning of Book XI Adam and Eve stand "in lowliest plight repentant," for prevenient grace, descending, has "remov'd/ The stonie from thir hearts" (1-4).[7] Milton

---

[6] *Ibid.*, pp. 43-45.

[7] In the judgment of early commentators—for example, Pearce and Greenwood—"stood" in line 1 meant "remained," as in "stand in arms." See Newton's gloss on xi, 1 in his London, 1778 edition of Milton's poems (Greenwood's comment did not appear in 1749). This reading may be correct; but Milton's sense of propriety may have been satisfied by prostration followed by manly erectness. In x, 1,099 the Parents are clearly prostrate. One ought, however, to note the contrary implication in xi, 148-50.

sees them as open, defenseless, like children who wait with averted faces for the punishment of confessed misbehavior. Yet with confession they have regained a part of their forfeited dignity:

> thir port
> Not of mean suiters, nor important less
> Seemd thir Petition
>
> (XI, 8-10)

than when Deucalion and Pyrrha, in fable, "before the Shrine/ Of *Themis* stood devout" (13-14).

This is one of many classical parallels which require the reader to bring to his sensing of the poem images laid up from earlier literary experience.[8] In Ovid's telling of the Deucalion story (*Metamorphoses*, I, 375-76) we learn that the Greek pair, on approaching the muddied shrine, fell prone on the ground and kissed the cold stones fearfully: *procumbit uterque/ pronus humi gelidoque pavens dedit oscula saxo*. An especially interesting point of contact, because when considered rationally it appears grotesque, is between the dampness caused by Ovid's flood and the wetting of the ground by Adam's and Eve's tears. Milton had written, "prostrate fell/ Before [God] reverent . . . and pardon begd, with tears/ Watering the ground" (X, 1,099-1,102). A second and deeper parallelism of situation is that, like the Biblical pair, Deucalion and Pyrrha were at the moment of praying the only two human beings on earth. Although thrust back out of prominence a third parallelism has to do with a similarity of result. "If by just prayers," say Deucalion and Pyrrha, praying together as Adam and Eve have been shown doing in Book V, "the Powers may be persuaded and softened, if the wrath of the

---

[8] Davis P. Harding's *The Club of Hercules: Studies in the Classical Background of Paradise Lost*, Urbana, Ill.: University of Illinois Press, 1962, has made much of this expectation.

gods may be turned aside, say, Themis, in what way the destruction of our race may be repaired, and lend thy help, O most mild one, to a flooded (*or* ruined) world."[9] The goddess is moved and gives instructions that the survivors should veil their heads, loosen their garments—presumably as a symbol of accessibility to divine commands or because the act was to result in a kind of generation like that usually accomplished in childbed—and throw stones over their shoulders, an act which will repeople the world. Adam and Eve also pray in a ruined world, for Milton regards their sin as no less catastrophic than Deucalion's flood; and their prayer also effects a kind of restoration.

Allusions of this kind, which are frequent in Milton's poem, evidently have rational and affective implications as well as perceptual. As visual image, however, the comparison is relevant because Deucalion and Pyrrha also are the sole human figures in the landscape, because each pair has prostrated itself, and because the attitude of each bespeaks entreaty. The initial impetus to the comparison may however have been a subcortical sensing of the dampness created by the Biblical Parents' watering of the ground with tears. Deucalion and Pyrrha had approached a shrine fouled by the detritus of a flood; Milton perceived a tactual likeness to the Ovidian scene without realizing that he did so and went on from there. No good reason exists why we should be contemptuous of such perceptions, for they are a part of the total human experience which the good poet is especially adept at rendering in its full concreteness.

The openness and defenselessness I have mentioned characterize Adam's attitude throughout the remainder of the epic.

[9] *Si precibus, dixerunt, numina iustis/ victa remollescunt, si flectitur ira deorum,/ dic, Themi, qua generis damnum reparabile nostri/ arte sit, et mersis fer opem, mitissima, rebus.* Ovid, *Metamorphoses,* 1, 377-80. Besides the ambiguity of *mersis* we may note the suggestiveness, in this context, of *damnum.*

Adam has never been much given to self-seeking. Throughout *Paradise Lost* his lack of ego is as remarkable as the preponderance of ego in Satan. From this point on he hears, exclaims, wonders, and questions, always accepting what he learns like a docile pupil absorbing knowledge from a teacher who is trusted absolutely. His receptivity is balanced by the confidence of Michael, whose knowledge, because it is being supplied to him progressively by God ("reveale/ To *Adam* what shall come in future dayes,/ As I shall thee enlight'n"—xi, 113-15), is unqualified by any self-doubt. On the one hand the posture and manner of the authoritative teacher, on the other those of the deferential pupil: these are the attitudinal poles of Books XI and XII which determine the large-scale structure. They have been determined in the first paragraph of Book XI by means as much perceptual as ideational.

Between Adam's prayer and the first vision he is shown from the specular mount, percepts continue to play a role. Because my intention is to focus chiefly on the revelations of man's unhappy future, I notice in passing only those which involve Adam directly. Since praying, he tells Eve, "Methought I saw him (God) placable and mild,/ Bending his eare" (xi, 151-52)—a visible embodiment of kindness. Eve's humble reply is spoken "with sad demeanour meek" (xi, 162), in a manner which expresses visually and tonally her improved spiritual state. Both parents next perceive indications of important alterations in Paradise; the air darkens, the eagle drives two lesser birds before him, the lion pursues a pair of deer. Adam infers correctly that "some furder change awaits us nigh" (xi, 193). The glorious apparition of Michael and his attendant angels on a hill is not sensed as glorious by Adam, for "carnal fear that day dimmd" (xi, 212) his eye. Michael approaches, "not unperceav'd" (xi, 224), and is recognized "by his Gate" (xi, 230) as an important angel; yet his "Majestie" is neither terrible nor sociably mild, like Raphael's, but "solemn and sublime" (xi, 232-36). When Adam bows low, "hee Kingly from his State/ Inclin'd not" (xi, 249-50). At the news that he and Eve are to be expelled from Paradise, Adam stands frozen to rigidity ("Heart-strook with chilling gripe of sorrow stood,/ That all his senses bound" (xi, 264-65). After Eve's lament from her hiding-place and Michael's reply, Adam's scattered animal spirits return and he addresses Michael humbly (xi, 294-95), his demeanor expressing acceptance. He recalls visits from the Divine Presence:

> On this Mount he appeerd, under this Tree
> Stood visible, among these Pines his voice
> I heard . . .
> In yonder nether World where shall I seek
> His bright appearances, or footstep trace?
> (xi, 320-29)

Michael again replies, and in the next paragraph the ocular visions begin. In this rapid summary much has of course been omitted; but enough has been said to indicate that Milton has continued to offer images as well as ideas.

The first vision is of the sacrifices offered by Abel and Cain and the subsequent murder of Abel. We are presented with a field, with sheaves, with an altar, and then

> thither anon
> A sweatie Reaper from his Tillage brought
> First Fruits, the green Eare, and the yellow Sheaf,
> Unculld, as came to hand; a Shepherd next
> More meek came with the Firstlings of his Flock
> Choicest and best; then sacrificing, laid
> The Inwards and thir Fat, with Incense strewd,
> On the cleft Wood, and all due Rites performd.
> His Offring soon propitious Fire from Heav'n
> Consum'd with nimble glance, and grateful steame;

The others not, for his was not sincere;
Whereat hee inlie rag'd, and as they talkd,
Smote him into the Midriff with a stone
That beat out life; he fell, and deadly pale
Groand out his Soul with gushing bloud effus'd.
Much at that sight was *Adam* in his heart
Dismaid . . .

(XI, 433-49)

A careful look at this excerpt will indicate both some of the opportunities and some of the drawbacks of the plan to present a large part of humankind's miserable history in visions.

First of all, we observe that the technique is cinematographic. The anticipation of panoramic photography need not perplex us, for in life we often see things at a distance, as Adam and Michael do here from a hilltop. Adam's vision, moreover, has been sharpened "with Euphrasie and Rue/ . . . And from the Well of Life three drops instilld" (XI, 414-16). Although we are not told that his hearing has been made preternaturally acute, we shall find as we proceed that he can hear too: for instance, Abel's dying groans and Noah's preaching. So far as possible, meanings are to be made visible, but the situation permits also oral glosses by Michael. There are no closeups; at no point does a face or a clenched fist or a pair of praying hands fill the mental screen. This is natural enough, for breadth of vision normally increases with distance, and Adam is a long way off. Consequently, a certain coolness is built into the selected technique. Because of the physical separation of observer and event, the aesthetic distance is unusually great.

Nevertheless we can clearly see meanings. Since Cain comes "sweatie" from his tillage he evidently has worked hard. We note that in placing his offerings on the altar he does not choose carefully but accepts the first that come to hand, "the green Eare, and the yellow Sheaf,/ Unculld," the unripe heads along with those that make the sheaf predominantly yellow. In contrast Abel brings "the Firstlings of his Flock/ Choicest and best." Presumably we watch him selecting; or perhaps we observe that all the chosen animals are unblemished. We may wonder, however, at Adam's lack of surprise that Abel should wish to kill some of the animals with which we have seen the Parents living in tolerant friendliness. So far as we know, the butchering of animals for food is outside Adam's experience. Also, the pace of the tableau is unrealistically rapid. Either the action is speeded up, as in some moving pictures, or Adam is given glimpses of actions at successive stages. The killing of the sacrificial animals and the dressing of them for offering ("laid/ The Inwards and thir Fat, with Incense strewd,/ On the cleft Wood") would in life take some time, and the other "due Rites" would take more. In the vision everything happens as quickly as the verse can inform us of it.

The rejection by God of one offering and his acceptance of the other causes some difficulty. The animals are "Consum'd with nimble glance, and grateful steame," with flames which gleam, dart, and, in burning, produce aromatic vapors that gratify God, or Abel, or both and must also be smelled by Adam and Michael despite their distance. (Otherwise the odor should not have been mentioned.) Or does "grateful" imply merely a visible eagerness in the flames to lick up the flesh? Cain's offering is not consumed. In any other circumstances this would be expected, for agricultural products offered to gods are not usually burned.[10] The King James account reads, "the Lord had respect unto Abel and to his offering: But unto Cain and to his offering he had not respect" (*Genesis* 4:4-5). Milton's problem was to render the lack of respect visible, and for this purpose he adopted a flame he had perhaps seen in Biblical paintings. Evidently

---

[10] But see *Leviticus* 2:1-3. I owe this reference to a student, William Miller.

the two offerings are set apart on the altar so that a tongue of fire can consume one in an ostentatiously selective way. On the whole the description works, at least on most readings. When I dwell on it, I confess I wish that the grain had been rejected in some other way, as, for instance, by a scattering wind.

Neither is Milton at top form in showing Cain's psychological processes. We are told, in a bald authorial gloss which runs directly counter to the narrative conditions Milton himself has determined, that Cain's offering was scorned because "his was not sincere." Several easy means were at hand to avoid the direct assertion of a state of mind not implied by sensory data. The comment could have been reserved for Michael to make later; or a perceptual basis for it could have been provided by juxtaposing it with "sweatie" and "Unculld," so that we could have inferred insincerity from Cain's failure to prepare himself for sacrifice by bathing as well as from his carelessness in choosing fruits; or some additional visual equivalent for insincerity could have been added before Michael's gloss. As things are, Milton simply ceases to describe, causes the epic voice to explain something, and then returns to description. Though the matter is not weighty, we have, I think, every right to cry "Fault!" *Bonus dormitat Homerus.* The technique recovers quickly. At the rejection of his offering Cain "inlie rag'd"—suppressed anger is easily enough shown visually—"and as they talkd,/ Smote (Abel) into the Midriff with a stone/ That beat out life." Like the fire, the stone was not Biblical but was not Milton's invention. Cowley, in Book I of *Davideis* (1656), had had Cain throw a stone at Abel

> as if he meant,
> At once his *Murder,* and his *Monument.*

From such frigid ingenuity as this Milton's description is

happily free. Yet the hurry of the summary forbids the giving of more than a minimal description and thus requires the pointing of significance by dialogue, which varies from relatively brief, as after this passage, to protracted.

Many of the visions resemble this first one in rapidity and spareness. But at times the poet's imagination is quickened by some appealing detail over which it is drawn to linger. This happens notably in the treatment of two unpromising verses in the Biblical source.

The first is *Genesis* 4:21, which says of Jubal, a descendant in the sixth generation from Cain, that "he was the father of all such as handle the harp and organ." Milton writes

> the sound
> Of Instruments that made melodious chime
> Was heard, of Harp and Organ; and who moovd
> Thir stops and chords was seen: his volant touch
> Instinct through all proportions low and high
> Fled and persu'd transverse the resonant fugue.
>
> (XI, 558-63)

The description of the fugue is modestly, and justly, famous. An encyclopaedia article on the fugue quotes it;[11] James Whaler praises it for its accuracy;[12] Sigmund Spaeth calls it "masterly."[13] The fingers fly ("volant") through varying harmonies in the bass and treble clefs ("all proportions low and high"), inspired, as it were, by a divine afflatus (*instinctus*, "impelled," as if by divine inspiration, *instinctu divino*), while the melodic line runs back and forth across the keyboard ("transverse") as though in flight and pursuit (whence the name, from *fuga*, "flight"). The image is auditory because

---

[11] *Encyclopaedia Britannica*, 1944, art. "fugue."

[12] James Whaler, "Counterpoint and Symbol: An Inquiry into the Rhythm of Milton's Epic Style," *Anglistica*, Vol. 6, Copenhagen: 1956, p. 75.

[13] Sigmund Spaeth, *Milton's Knowledge of Music*, Princeton: The University Library, 1913, p. 47.

sound is being described, but it is auditory also because the words are themselves musical sound. The space given to Jubal may seem, to a coldly logical judgment, excessive. It was traditional, however, for a story of origins like Milton's to describe the beginnings of arts and crafts, as Lucretius had done in *De Rerum Natura* and Du Bartas in his *Sepmaines*.

The development of *Genesis* 4:22, "And Zillah, she also bare Tubal-cain, an instructor of every artificer in brass and iron," has to do precisely with crafts. The means are again mainly sensory, presentational. We are shown Tubal-cain at the forge draining liquid ore into moulds to make at first tools and later "what might else be wrought/ Fusil or grav'n in mettle" (xi, 572-73). True, we are given alternative explanations of where the metal may have come from:

> (whether found where casual fire
> Had wasted woods on Mountain or in Vale,
> Down to the veins of Earth, thence gliding hot
> To some Caves mouth, or whether washt by stream
> From underground) . . .
>
> (xi, 566-70)

In reading, however, we have glimpses of forest fires, denuded areas on mountain or in valley, hot streams of metal, and rivers discharging lumps of ore above ground. The offering of alternatives was also solidly in the epic tradition; Lucretius had used them (although not the same two as Milton) in his account of the development of the metal crafts (*De Rerum Natura*, v, 1,241-96). Along with the spreading of sin after the Fall there had been a simultaneous progress in means by which hardship might be lightened. These belonged in Milton's summary also, although not much room could be allowed them, for they cross the generally downward tendency of the narrative with a thin upcurve of hope.

At one other point in Book XI a vision notably expands a

Biblical text. *Genesis* 6:2 has "the sons of God saw the daughters of men that they were fair; and they took them wives of all which they chose." Milton's sensory equivalent runs as follows:

> from the Tents behold
> A Beavie of fair Women, richly gay
> In Gems and wanton dress; to the Harp they sung
> Soft amorous Ditties, and in dance came on:
> The Men though grave, ey'd them, and let thir eyes
> Rove without rein, till in the amorous Net
> Fast caught, they lik'd, and each his liking chose;
> And now of love they treat till th' Eevning Starr
> Loves Harbinger appeerd; then all in heat
> They light the Nuptial Torch, and bid invoke
> *Hymen*, then first to marriage Rites invok't;
> With Feast and Musick all the Tents resound.
> Such happy interview and fair event
> Of love and youth not lost, Songs, Garlands, Flours,
> And charming Symphonies attachd the heart
> Of *Adam*, soon enclin'd to admit delight . . .
> (XI, 581-96)

No doubt certain phrases should be read with a scornful curl of the lips: "Beavie," "wanton dress," "in the amorous Net/ Fast caught," and perhaps others. Adam, however, is seeing, not hearing, and as yet his inexperience does not permit him to suspect evil in what is outwardly fair. The amorous net is a favorite image; it will reappear in the "snare," the "ginns, and toils" of *Samson Agonistes* (931, 933) and again in the "Amorous Nets" of *Paradise Regained* (II, 162). Its point, of course, is that female charm has a tendency softly to envelop the susceptible male and render him helpless. The net cannot appear in the vision, only the insinuating graces which it metaphorizes. The appearance of a metaphor in the description of a vision deserves remark because such metaphors are comparatively rare in this book. "All in heat/ They light the Nuptial Torch" contains another, but less obtrusive, one. For the rest, Michael plays fair in presenting the vision and Milton in describing it, so that the ensuing commentary must explain that the tents are tents of wickedness (XI, 607-608) and that the fair female troop is "empty of all good wherein consists/ Womans domestic honour and chief praise" (XI, 616-17). Like the other two passages which expand the Biblical source, this one awakens in the poet a special kind of interest. Milton could never write coldly about the power of coquettish triviality to seduce unwary wisdom.

Elsewhere the visions either generalize human sufferings or contract sacred history by cramming a number of events into a tight summary. The earliest generalizing vision is that of the lazar-house, "wherein were laid/ Numbers of all diseas'd, all maladies/ Of gastly Spasm, or racking torture, qualmes/ Of heart-sick Agonie" (XI, 479-82)—and fifteen other named maladies. The structurally determinant word is "all"; having used it, Milton is committed to embark on a catalogue, which cannot really be exhaustive but will suffice to illustrate adequately the kinds of things meant to be included. After the list of particulars the passage reverts to generalities:

> Dire was the tossing, deep the groans, despair
> Tended the sick busiest from Couch to Couch;
> And over them triumphant Death his Dart
> Shook, but delaid to strike.
>
> (XI, 489-92)

No matter what their special ailments, all the sick were in pain and felt mental agony as they waited for death.

The vision of war is similarly general. Soldiers are shown doing all the things they do typically.

Part wield thir Arms, part curb the foaming Steed,
Single or in Array of Battel rang'd
Both Horse and Foot, nor idely mustring stood;
One way a Band select from forage drives
A herd of Beeves, faire Oxen and faire Kine
From a fat Meddow ground . . .
                    Others to a Citie strong
Lay Siege, encampt; by Batterie, Scale, and Mine,
Assaulting; others from the Wall defend
With Dart and Jav'lin, Stones and sulfurous Fire;
On each hand slaughter and gigantic deeds.
                    (xi, 643-59)

This is no particular war but War itself, freed of limiting
circumstances and presented as an archetype. The summary
ends, "so Violence/ Proceeded, and Oppression, and Sword-
Law/ Through all the Plain, and refuge none was found"
(xi, 671-73). When the emphasis shifts to the corruptions of
peace, again the images are of classes of activities:

All now was turnd to jollitie and game,
To luxurie and riot, feast and dance,
Marrying or prostituting, as befell,
Rape or Adulterie, where passing faire
Allur'd them; thence from Cups to civil Broiles.
                    (xi, 714-18)

The temporal equivalence of description and image is
destroyed. The phrase "Marrying or prostituting, as befell"
could be expanded by a moving picture director into a whole
series of successive dramas; and so with most of the other
phrases. The pressure of business allows only blurred glimpses
of moral corruption.

The visual summaries of Biblical history are qualitatively
different. We have paused on Cain's murder of Abel and

have space to consider a part of the Noah story. When Noah perceived the uselessness of his exhortations against corruption, he

> remov'd his Tents farr off;
> Then from the Mountain hewing Timber tall,
> Began to build a Vessel of huge bulk,
> Measur'd by Cubit, length, and bredth, and highth,
> Smeard round with Pitch, and in the side a dore
> Contriv'd, and of provisions laid in large
> For Man and Beast: when loe a wonder strange!
> Of everie Beast, and Bird, and Insect small
> Came seav'ns, and pairs, and enterd in, as taught
> Thir order; last the Sire, and his three Sons
> With thir four Wives; and God made fast the dore.
> Meanwhile the Southwind rose, and with black wings
> Wide hovering, all the Clouds together drove
> From under Heav'n; the Hills to their supplie
> Vapour, and Exhalation dusk and moist,
> Sent up amain; and now the thick'nd Skie
> Like a dark Ceeling stood; down rushd the Rain
> Impetuous, and continu'd till the Earth
> No more was seen; the floating Vessel swum
> Uplifted; and secure with beaked prow
> Rode tilting ore the Waves; all dwellings else
> Flood overwhelmd, and them with all thir pomp
> Deep under water rould; Sea coverd Sea,
> Sea without shoar; and in thir Palaces
> Where luxurie late reignd, Sea-monsters whelpd
> And stabl'd; of Mankind, so numerous late,
> All left, in one small bottom swum imbarkt.

(XI, 727-53)

This excerpt, finally, we must examine for perceptual content. First of all, we note again that the failure to exploit all the opportunities for visual development is a consequence of the need for brevity. For 851 words in *Genesis* 6:14-7:24, Milton has substituted only 208, or less than one-fourth the number. He dares not pause on details either of the ark's construction or of the ruin caused by the flood. "And all flesh died that moved upon the earth, both of fowl, and of cattle, and of beast, and of every creeping thing that creepeth upon the earth, and every man: All in whose nostrils was the breath of life, of all that was in the dry land, died" (*Genesis* 7:21-22). Of man Milton can only say, "All left, in one small bottom swum imbarkt," and of the fowl and cattle and wild beasts and serpents and insects he can say nothing at all. Yet the passage is by no means sensorially blank.

At the beginning the imagery is chiefly motor: "remov'd," "hewing," "build," "Measur'd," "Smeard," "Contriv'd," "laid in." Although the tension is minimal, if we read empathetically we note the tallness of the timber and the huge bulk of the gradually shaping hull and recognize the magnitude of Noah's task. The point must not be strained; Milton does not himself in imagination lay resounding strokes against the boles of towering trees but watches at a remove. Yet if he does not clamorously require us to share Noah's exertions, he permits us to realize that they must have been great. With "God made fast the dore" the muscular energy is increased— oddly, for the detail is Milton's, and unexpected. We infer that the securing of the entrance against wind and waves requires a strength greater than man's. Then comes the storm, and from this point to the end the verse surges and swells with the water. The black wings of the south wind hover across one line-ending, then, specifically as clouds, drive across another; and beginning with "the thick'nd Skie/ Like a dark Ceeling stood," seven consecutive lines have enjambment. The rain rushes down, the vessel swims uplifted and tilting, the dwellings are overwhelmed and roll with their pomp under deep water, sea monsters stable and whelp in once luxurious chambers. (Here the poet briefly gives us an aquanaut's view.) Of mankind, all that are left swim embarked in the "small bottom" which the vessel "of huge bulk" has become as it floats on a shoreless sea. The vision has started tamely but gathered momentum as it proceeded, until at the end the images are powerful enough to grip us. On the whole we may conclude that the perceptual content of the visions in Book XI is satisfactory. As was said earlier, Milton wrote before criticism had insisted that poetry show instead of telling, and he made no doctrinal commitment to fill his lines with images. Moreover, he had an unconscionable amount of subject matter to present, so that he had to keep his narrative spare. If at times he is the skilled pedagogue, complacently giving us valuable information in the fewest possible words, he is also, consistently, a stylist who offers images where they are appropriate. Given his narrative problem, it is perhaps unreasonable to expect him to have done more.

When we proceed to a consideration of affective content we notice at once that Adam's responses to the visions and Michael's comments on the responses afford rich opportunities for the embodiment of feelings. We have already encountered polar attitudes—feelings structured in such a way as to shape the perception of experiences—in Adam's submissiveness and Michael's confident authority; and many of the sensory data already noticed imply emotional meanings. These, although important, we shall have no time to examine, any more than we shall be able to pay much heed to perceptual content in the speeches of Michael and Adam. The discussion will thus be far short of exhaustive, since each of the chief material strands of Books XI and XII will be studied with relation to only one of our two major interests.

On the superficial level the books are filled with explicit

statements about affective reactions. Most of these have to do with Adam. That this is so ought not, of course, to make us feel that Michael is coldly unconcerned. After the first vision Milton writes of the angel, "hee also mov'd, repli'd" (xi, 453); and we are perhaps to spread this hint of involvement over the remainder of the narrative. Nevertheless the focus is quite properly on the human being whose sin has initiated the long history of suffering about which we are to learn.

> Much at that sight was *Adam* in his heart
> Dismaid . . .
>
> (xi, 448-49)

> O sight
> Of terrour, foul and ugly to behold,
> Horrid to think, how horrible to feel!
>
> (xi, 463-65)

> Sight so deform what heart of Rock could long
> Drie-ey'd behold? *Adam* could not, but wept.
>
> (xi, 494-95)

> I yeild it just, said *Adam*, and submit.
>
> (xi, 526)

> attachd the heart
> Of *Adam*, soon enclin'd to admit delight,
> The bent of Nature . . .
>
> (xi, 595-97)

> To whom thus *Adam* of short joy bereft.
> O pittie and shame . . .
>
> (xi, 628-29)

> *Adam* was all in tears, and to his guide
> Lamenting turnd full sad . . .
>
> (xi, 674-75)

O Visions ill foreseen! better had I
Liv'd ignorant of future. . .

(XI, 763-64)

Whereat the heart of *Adam* erst so sad
Greatly rejoyc'd . . .

(XI, 868-69)

Whereto thus *Adam* fatherly displeas'd.
(XII, 63)

This yet I apprehend not . . .

(XII, 280)

Adam with such joy
Surcharg'd, as had like grief bin dewd in tears
Without the vent of words . . .

(XII, 372-74)

our Sire
Replete with joy and wonder thus repli'd.
(XII, 467-68)

Greatly instructed I shall hence depart,
Greatly in peace of thought . . .

(XII, 557-58)

Although more excerpts could be given than these, the curve
of Adam's emotional experience in the two books has been
roughly indicated.

In the main, the knowledge given Adam of the future ap-
palls him, partly because the events are intrinsically horrible
and partly because of his acceptance of responsibility for
them. At times, through misunderstanding, he reacts joyfully
to what is only meretriciously good, as when he says "Much
better seems this Vision" (XI, 599) at the spectacle of the
grave men being seduced into marriage by the fair women.
His negative emotions of course vary from moment to mo-

ment—he is terrified, grieved, moved to pity and displeasure—
but before the prophecy of Christ's birth such relief as he
finds is temporary, and the blest Seer's predictions are generally depressing throughout nearly 600 lines (xi, 423, through
xii, 120). Thereafter a gradual rise begins with the promise
that from Abram a mighty nation will be raised (xii, 120-24),
and the curve continues gently upward to the description of
the Second Coming and Judgment, which evoke from Adam
the cry, "O goodness infinite, goodness immense!" (xii, 469).
Here occurs another dip in the quick summary of church
history: "Wolves shall succeed for teachers, grievous Wolves"
(xii, 508). By now, however, Adam has learned to swallow
huge chunks of future misery without losing his emotional
poise, and the total effect is to leave the peccant ancestor
"Greatly in peace of thought" (xii, 558). After a final summary by Michael the epic slopes into the conclusion already
discussed in Chapter III.

For several reasons the upward turn at the end is necessary:
because epic traditionally ended happily; because the Biblical
story in fact recorded a merciful intervention in human
calamities and implied a dénouement which would leave
permanently blissful all those human creatures who deserved
joy; and, not least important, because Milton sensed, as the
best writers have always done, that literature ought ultimately
to reconcile and strengthen, to return the audience to the
everyday world with enhanced willingness to meet the
stresses of living. Yet the general impression of readers appears
to be that the books are heavy and dry. We shall examine
the justice of the impression by looking very briefly at Book
XII, which has been slighted in the preceding pages, merely
pausing to observe once more that by restricting our view we
not only deprive ourselves of useful evidence but also choose
for emphasis the less promising half of our subject matter.

The five introductory lines to Book XII were added in

1674, when the former tenth book was divided; and here, at least, there can be no suspicion of coldness. Michael pauses to see "If *Adam* aught perhaps might interpose" (xii, 4). He is concerned about his listener, does not want to frustrate Adam's impulses to self-expression—and this despite the fact that he himself is "bent on speed" (xii, 2). When Adam remains silent, the archangel "with transition sweet new Speech resumes" (xii, 5). "Sweet" is exactly the adjective that is needed. What has been most wanting in Book XI is precisely sweetness. If the sweetness is partly in matter—"Thus thou hast seen one World begin and end;/ And Man as from a second stock proceed" (xii, 6-7)—we can hardly be mistaken in accepting it also as a quality of the angel's manner. The wait for a remark by Adam has been courteous, and so too is what Michael proceeds immediately to say:

> but I perceave
> Thy mortal sight to faile; objects divine
> Must needs impaire and wearie human sense.
> Henceforth what is to com I will relate.
>
> (xii, 8-11)

Michael is not the insensitive pedagogue who grinds through to the end of a prepared demonstration while his pupils' eyes glaze over. Milton feels here the strain of Adam's situation as C. S. Lewis, in *Perelandra*, feels that of Ransom, who in conversation with unseen Deity is forced by a sensation of intolerable weight to sit on the ground. As Lewis has remarked elsewhere, confrontation with Perfect Goodness combined with Absolute Power would be an overwhelming rather than a cozy experience; and on Adam Michael's visit has a similar, if less extreme, effect.

The transition from visions to narration causes an alteration in affective values. Newton quotes Addison's comment that "If Milton's poem flags any where, it is in this narration," and adds that "if we have an eye only to poetic decoration, his remark is just."[14] Yet if certain opportunities are renounced, others are opened up. Narration permits the admission of more judgmental phrases, and these always tend to give a recountal human warmth because they imply that the events have a leverage on feelings. Hitherto Michael's sensibility has had to restrain itself until Adam has reacted. Now commentary can begin to accompany the descriptions.

The technique gives rise to some awkwardness. In lines 101-102 Michael says, metaphorically we may think, "Witness th' irreverent Son/ Of him who built the Ark." By line 128 it appears that the visions are continuing for Michael, if not for Adam: "I see him, but thou canst not." Still later Adam is called on to observe settings, although not people and happenings: "See where it flows, disgorging at seav'n mouthes/ Into the Sea" (158-59); and "that proud Citie, whose high Walls thou sawst/ Left in confusion" (342-43); Adam has *not* seen them. Perhaps most interesting of all is Adam's speech, "now first I finde/ Mine eyes true op'ning" (273-74). The implication, as in other speeches about blindness (for example, III, 51-55, and *Samson Agonistes*, 1,687-89), that the mind may be illuminated without the aid of physical light, in this context is boldly paradoxical because Adam's eyes had been preternaturally open in Book XI and have "failed" since the beginning of Book XII. Nonetheless some doubt is thrown backward on Michael's "Henceforth what is to com I will relate." The usual interpretation is "From now on I will tell you about the future instead of showing it to you"; could the intended meaning have been rather "Because the visions pain your eyes, I will interpret for you those which are yet to come"? Since we have been told that Michael is to instruct Adam "As I shall thee enlight'n" (XI, 115), the visions may be produced not by Michael but by God (or the Son),

14 Newton's note on XII, 11.

and Michael may learn the future only as it is shown him.

In any event, Addison's judgment of Book XII need not be accepted without question. Thyer took a different view: the causing of Michael to see "as in vision, and give a rapturous inliven'd account" results in "great ease to the languishing attention of the reader."[15] Perhaps Book XII is somewhat more relaxed than Book XI because the reader is told more and hence need infer less; but this is appropriate, for Adam has by now recovered sufficiently from his original shock to be able to reflect more quietly, as he should do to assimilate the knowledge. The responses, however, are now divided more evenly between Adam and Michael, so that both are able to contribute to whatever emotional warmth the book may contain.

As in Book XI Adam's comments consistently show affective implication. But Michael's? It is in them, if anywhere, that dryness and bleakness must be found. Let us look at a sample passage—the description of Abram's journey to Canaan, where there is no special emotional tension. Rather the contrary, since Abram meets with no dramatic obstacles and the passage focuses chiefly on the naming of places.

> I see him, but thou canst not, with what Faith
> He leaves his Gods, his Friends, and native Soile
> *Ur* of *Chaldaea*, passing now the Ford
> To *Haran*, after him a cumbrous Train
> Of Herds and Flocks, and numerous servitude;
> Not wandring poor, but trusting all his wealth
> With God, who calld him, in a land unknown.
> *Canaan* he now attains, I see his Tents
> Pitcht about *Sechem*, and the neighbouring Plaine
> Of *Moreh*; there by promise he receaves
> Gift to his Progenie of all that Land;

[15] Quoted in Newton's note on XII, 128.

From *Hamath* Northward to the Desert South
(Things by thir names I call, though yet unnam'd)
From *Hermon* East to the great Western Sea,
Mount *Hermon*, yonder Sea, each place behold
In prospect, as I point them; on the shoare
Mount *Carmel*; here the double-founted stream
Jordan, true limit Eastward; but his Sons
Shall dwell to *Senir*, that long ridge of Hills.
This ponder, that all Nations of the Earth
Shall in his Seed be blessed; by that Seed
Is meant thy great deliverer, who shall bruise
The Serpents head; whereof to thee anon
Plainlier shall be reveald.

(XII, 128-51)

The announcement that the deliverer will come of Abram's seed is very laconic, but only because more will be said of Christ later. For the rest, the passage is spoken calmly but is not without indications that Michael is deeply engrossed in his subject.

The evidence is quite clear. "I see him . . . with what Faith/ He leaves his Gods, his Friends, and native Soile": Michael feels wondering approval. "Not wandring poor, but trusting all his wealth/ With God, who calld him, in a land unknown": the risk is discerned, the faith again commended. "Each place behold/ In prospect, as I point them": the Archangel is eager for attention, glances to see whether Adam is watching, stretches an arm toward Sechem, Moreh, Hamath, the southern desert, Mount Hermon (having said simply "Hermon," he goes back to be more helpful and says "Mount *Hermon*"), Mount Carmel, Jordan, Senir, "that long ridge of Hills." The *cicerone* is not bored. His insistence on detail implies an expectation of strong curiosity in his listener, and that in turn implies his own interest. "This ponder" suggests, as Newton observed, "I mention other things for your information, but this you should particularly remember, and meditate upon."[16] If what precedes has been significant, this is more so. The lack of urgency in sound, metrics, and diction is partly compensated by syntactical stress. Christ's coming can be mentioned here, and even said to be worth pondering, but the lack of strong affective emphasis is intended. The climax of all the revelations cannot yet be given its full emotional value.

Other parts of Michael's narrative also carry affective overtones. Not all—the Archangel's hurry forces him at times so to compress his recital that there is room for little but the bare events. After Joseph's death, the Israelites become

> Suspected to a sequent King, who seeks
> To stop thir overgrowth, as inmate guests
> Too numerous; whence of guests he makes them slaves
> Inhospitably, and kills thir infant Males:
> Till by two brethren (those two brethren call
> *Moses* and *Aaron*) sent from God to claime
> His people from enthralment, they return
> With glory and spoile back to thir promisd Land.
>
> (xii, 165-72)

Except for "Inhospitably" and "With glory and spoile," the passage is composed of mere facts; and the latter phrase is careless, for Milton did not really think that glory should be linked with the acquisition of spoils. The poet is left uneasy (partly because of the slip?) and retraces his steps:

> But first the lawless Tyrant, who denies
> To know thir God, or message to regard,
> Must be compelld by Signes and Judgements dire . . .
>
> (xii, 173-75)

---

[16] Newton's note on xii, 147.

The disapproval is evident. In the following forty and a half lines the discussion of signs and judgments includes frequent attitudinal notations ("loath'd," "submits," "Humbles," "as Ice/ More hard'nd after thaw," "rage," "Aw'd," "wondrous," "obdurat," "trouble"). We may guess that throughout Books XI and XII Milton was torn between a desire to hurry, to get on with his story and round out his epic, and a subconscious realization that too much compression would result in frigidity. If his compromise was not always equally happy, it is regularly workmanlike and yields increasing evidences of warmth to reexamination.

From about line 270 the emotional intensity mounts. God's favoring of the Israelites and his ultimate sending of a Redeemer who will bruise the head of Satan and defeat Sin and Death, whom we have seen in Book X entering the world to lick up its draff and filth, are the events toward which the entire recital has pointed. The triumph is the greater because the calamities have been heavy; if the description had harrowed us less, the relief would have been less welcome. Adam's joy ("O goodness infinite, goodness immense!/ That all this good of evil shall produce," 469-70) has been sufficiently discussed by others, as has also the skill with which Milton has given his cosmic tragedy the happy issue appropriate to epic. Our relief as we approach the end is not unalloyed. The warning that wolves shall succeed the disciples as teachers and that "heavie persecution shall arise/ On all who in the worship persevere/ Of Spirit and Truth" (xii, 508, 531-33) tones the satisfaction with sadness.

In the final thirteen lines the poignancy is wonderfully tender.

> In either hand the hastning Angel caught
> Our lingring Parents, and to th' Eastern Gate
> Led them direct, and down the Cliff as fast

To the subjected Plaine; then disappeerd.
They looking back, all th' Eastern side beheld
Of Paradise, so late thir happie seat,
Wav'd over by that flaming Brand, the Gate
With dreadful Faces throngd and fierie Armes:
Som natural tears they dropd, but wip'd them soon;
The World was all before them, where to choose
Thir place of rest, and Providence thir guide:
They hand in hand with wandring steps and slow,
Through *Eden* took thir solitarie way.

(xii, 637-49)

Reluctant to leave what until the commission of sin had been their happy seat, the Parents hang back as Michael leads them by the hand out the eastern gate and down to the plain. Longfellow, in a sonnet called "Nature," describes a domestic situation of a similar though lower-keyed sort.

As a fond mother, when the day is o'er,
　Leads by the hand her little child to bed,
　Half willing, half reluctant to be led,
　And leave his broken playthings on the floor,
Still gazing at them through the open door,
　Nor wholly reassured and comforted
　By promises of others in their stead,
　Which, though more splendid, may not please
　　him more . . .

In neither passage is the urgency of the leader unkind; and in both firmness is softened by a physical contact which implies love. Michael does not drive Adam and Eve out of the Garden ahead of him but walks out with them holding each by one hand, so that although they are separated by him they are also joined through him—and we may remember that as God's messenger he stands, in some sense, for God.

223

When, at the bottom of the hill, the Parents look back for a last glimpse of their former home, they see not only "the Eastern side" but also, frighteningly, a flaming sword and the dreadful faces and fiery weapons of the angelic guard whose mission is to prevent their return. No resumption of their former life is possible; its very locale is closed off, locked against them, forever. They "drop" some natural tears—the significance of their dropping, instead of shedding, the tears was commented on in Chapter III—but wipe their eyes with hands or hair. The action is a symbol of acceptance, and they turn next to the world which lies "before them." It is wide, full of opportunities and perhaps also of dangers, but Providence will be their guide in it. We remember that Michael had said in Book XI, "Doubt not but in Vallie and in Plaine/ God is as here, and will be found alike/ Present" (XI, 349-51).

Little now remains to be done. Hand in hand, with slow and uncertain steps which show not only reluctance and perplexity but also a willingness to meet whatever experiences may lie ahead, Adam and Eve proceed "solitarie," but not abandoned, through a plain which although not Paradise is still Eden. The movement is toward Milton and his seventeenth century readers and toward us, who, as we close the book, are warmed by the knowledge that as God did not withdraw his love from our erring Parents, so the poet, at the end of his exhausting task, has not been drawn by his acquiescence to God's justice either to perceive the unfortunate human situation dimly or to feel it coldly.

The topics listed here are a selection of those discussed in the text. The names are of real persons (and Homer), not of Biblical or fictive characters. Thus Lucretius and Bishop Thomas Newton appear, but not Adam or Ithuriel. Although titles like *Hamlet* and Aristotle's *Poetics* are listed, modern critical writings must be sought under their authors' names.

It has not seemed useful to list cited Miltonic passages by book and line number or by key word. Except in Chapters I-III, the position of most is determined by the following system: from Books I and II, Chapter IV; from Books III and IV, Chapter V; from Books V and VI, Chapter VI; from Books VII and VIII, Chapter VII; from Books IX and X, Chapter VIII; from Books XI and XII, Chapter IX.